Untrodden Ways

Untrodden Ways

A Guide to Some of Britain's Lesser-known
Long-distance Footpaths

Nick Channer

WARD LOCK

A Ward Lock Book

First published in the UK 1991
by Ward Lock
(a Cassell imprint)
Villiers House
41/47 Strand
LONDON
WC2N 5JE

Distributed in the United States
by Sterling Publishing Co., Inc.
387 Park Avenue South, New York, NY 10016–8810
Distributed in Australia
by Capricorn Link (Australia) Pty Ltd
P.O. Box 665, Lane Cove, NSW 2066

Jacket photograph: The Seven Sisters
from the Vanguard Way (Maurice and Joyce Fowler).

British Library Cataloguing in Publication Data
Channer, Nick
Untrodden Ways : A Guide to Some of Britain's Lesser-known
Long-distance Footpaths
1. Great Britain. Footpaths – Visitors' guides
I. Title
914.104859
ISBN 0-7063-7056-2

Typeset by Columns Design and Production Services Ltd, Reading

Printed and bound in Spain by Graficromo

Contents

She dwelt among the untrodden ways
    Beside the springs of Dove
A maid whom there were none to praise
    And very few to love:

A violet by a mossy stone
    Half hidden from the eye!
Fair as a star, when only one
    Is shining in the sky.

She lived unknown, and few could know
    When Lucy ceased to be;
But she is in her grave, and, oh,
    The difference to me!

William Wordsworth, 1800

Introduction

Walking is now Britain's most popular outdoor leisure activity, with new footpaths springing into existence all the time and new ramblers to tread them. But next time you are out walking in the countryside, spare a thought for how it all began.

On 24 April 1965 a major battle was won, a classic example of triumph over adversity. Its participants comprised protective landowners, faceless government figures and single-minded outdoor enthusiasts. At Malham Tarn House in North Yorkshire on that memorable spring day, the Pennine Way was officially opened. A red-letter day indeed, witnessing the most important achievement in the history of the Ramblers' Association (RA) for at last Britain's first national long-distance footpath was established.

It was the brainchild of Tom Stephenson, the grand master of the rambling world and one-time secretary of the Association. As a child, he had roamed the wild uplands and bleak, barren expanses of the Pennines, gazing in wide-eyed bewilderment at the forbidden tracts of land and the gamekeepers who often blocked his path. 'I could never understand how anyone could own a mountain,' he wrote later. 'Surely it was there for everybody.' It was among these dark, desolate moors that a dream was kindled in Stephenson's mind, a dream that was to become the Pennine Way.

In a 1935 article in the *Daily Herald* headed, 'Wanted – a Long Green Trail', he described the thinking behind his seemingly simple objective. Little did he know that it would take thirty years to realize his dream. During those long years of wrangling and recrimination, there were countless prosecutions for trespassing and prison sentences were handed out. Nevertheless, week after week huge armies of ramblers invaded the prohibited moorlands, regardless of the consequences. They had only one aim in mind – to win. At times the fight seemed endless and the prospect of victory more remote with each passing year. Landowners had seen it all before, of course. In April 1932, 500 ramblers flooded on to Kinder Scout in Derbyshire to argue the right of public access to the countryside.

The National Parks and Access to the Countryside Act of 1949 helped the cause of the RA in no small way. As a consequence of the Act, national parks were developed and definitive rights of way established. Public access was here to stay among the windswept fells and moorland sweeps. Even today, though, in the 1990s, the battle is still continuing. Forbidden Britain Day is the RA's annual attempt to draw attention to the ongoing problems of restricted access to the countryside, but unlike in those far-off days when Tom Stephenson battled to establish the Pennine Way, today the RA has a new and invaluable weapon with which to fire its broadsides – the media.

So that takes care of the Pennine Way and the roots of today's flourishing walking industry. In its wake, of course, other long-distance footpaths have been set up, and the Countryside Commission is now responsible for more than twelve such routes, including Offa's Dyke, the Ridgeway and the South West Peninsula Coast Path. The Commission proposes to adopt more routes in the future, but the process is always slow and protracted, so who knows what may happen. It has been suggested that the routes should be renamed 'national trails'. This would do justice to their international and domestic importance for tourism, but then, that is another issue entirely.

★

To focus on the specific long-distance paths chosen for this book, they are not as illustrious as those I have already mentioned, though some have similar status or patronage. There are numerous publications dealing with these well-known long-distance walks and there is understandable scepticism about the need for yet more guides on the subject. However, with serious erosion occurring on many of these routes, there is mounting pressure to highlight some of the country's other, lesser-known, paths – our 'untrodden ways'.

This does not mean that the walks I have chosen here are not established paths over public rights of way. Some have deservedly been recognized by county councils, as in the case of the recently opened Heart of England Way, and a few have even been pioneered by local authority bodies. Others have been devised by individuals, groups of enthusiasts and rambling clubs.

At best they are excellent, well-maintained paths, clearly waymarked with good route-finding instructions. In some cases, moorland paths are not easily defined and, here, a good

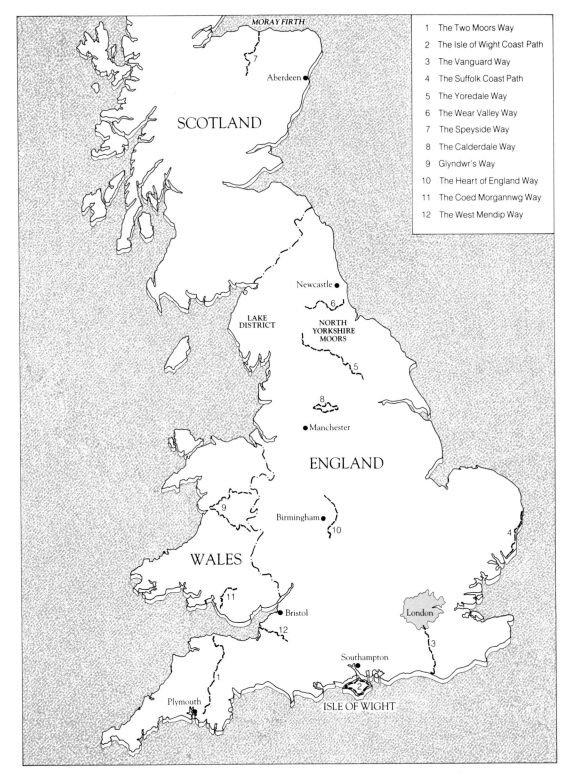

MORAY FIRTH

7

Aberdeen ●

SCOTLAND

	1	The Two Moors Way
	2	The Isle of Wight Coast Path
	3	The Vanguard Way
	4	The Suffolk Coast Path
	5	The Yoredale Way
	6	The Wear Valley Way
	7	The Speyside Way
	8	The Calderdale Way
	9	Glyndwr's Way
	10	The Heart of England Way
	11	The Coed Morgannwg Way
	12	The West Mendip Way

Newcastle ●

6

LAKE
DISTRICT

NORTH
YORKSHIRE
MOORS

5

8

● Manchester

ENGLAND

9

Birmingham ●
10

4

WALES

11

● Bristol

12

London

3

Southampton

1

2

Plymouth

ISLE OF WIGHT

compass is recommended. One or two routes can be a bit of an obstacle course – infrequently signposted, overgrown in places or simply neglected. But all this is part of the challenge of undertaking the walk – you take the rough with the smooth.

To include all the less-familiar paths here would be impossible; there now exists a vast network of them throughout the country – more than 400 at the last count. What I have done instead is to select those routes which I consider are both representative of the entire stock and, perhaps more importantly, capture the true spirit and character of the British countryside – everything from the banks of a famous salmon river in Scotland to a popular sunshine island off the south coast.

It is possible to divide some of these long-distance paths into distinct categories. For example, the topography of the Two Moors Way (Chapter 1) in the West Country is similar in some respects to the Yoredale Way (Chapter 5) in North Yorkshire. They both cross soft but spectacular tracts of moorland interspersed with lovely villages of quaint cottages. Waterfalls and wooded ravines abound. Interestingly, both walks have a fondness for national parks. The Two Moors Way begins on the southern edge of Dartmoor and finishes where Exmoor, the smallest of all the national parks, meets the Bristol Channel. The Yoredale Way, on the other hand, initially follows the gentle waters of the River Ure as it meanders through the fertile Vale of York. At length the path journeys to the Yorkshire Dales National Park, that delightful region of the country so lovingly portrayed in the books of James Herriot. Here, the scenery is soft and rolling, with distant sweeps of fell and an occasional glimpse of the towering Pennines, the path's final objective.

The Wear Valley Way (Chapter 6) in the north-east of England and the Coed Morgannwg Way (Chapter 11) in South Wales have a wonderfully atmospheric flavour to them, with their lead and coal-mining associations. Surrounded by dramatic, windswept hills and belts of dense, dark forest, they abound with the ghosts of the past, when these landscapes were filthy black with industry.

The Calderdale Way (Chapter 8) is rugged too, with the path following the contours of the Calder Valley. In places its Pennine setting is somewhat bleak and inhospitable, and there are frequent reminders of the valley's vital role in the Industrial Revolution.

Glyndwr's Way (Chapter 9) runs through the remote sheep-farming country of mid-Wales, rich in legend and folklore, and here the surroundings are enhanced by the haunting beauty of a ruined abbey or a spectacular man-made lake sheltering under wooded hills and moors. It was in this fabled district that Owain Glyndwr battled in bloody fashion for an independent Wales in the fifteenth century.

The Speyside Way (Chapter 7) on the north-east shoulder of
Scotland does not always conform to the typical concept of
Scottish scenery. In its early and middle stages the path runs
along the broad valley of this noble salmon river, through a
land of ospreys, soft burn water, peat and barley, with only the
merest inkling of far-off majestic peaks. Lovers of high-
mountain grandeur take heart. By the end of the walk, you
are in familiar territory at the foot of the Cairngorms and
hopefully content.

The Heart of England Way (Chapter 10) cuts a green swath
through the West Midlands, encountering various rivers, canals
and fine country houses and acting as a sort of symbolic border
between the rugged splendour of the north and the gentler,
more placid south and east of England.

The Suffolk Coast Path (Chapter 4) follows an extraordinarily
isolated, rather sad and yet fascinating stretch of historic,
crumbling coastline – the sinister sanctuary of prosperous
smugglers. The whole region has a delightfully nostalgic feel
about it.

The Isle of Wight (Chapter 2), on the other hand, is a bright,
bustling place, modern and lively, with its own inimitable
personality. Like Suffolk, coastal erosion is a serious problem
here, as the sea steadily encroaches upon the land.

The Vanguard Way (Chapter 3) is an interesting long-
distance path, attempting to pack in as much variety as it can.
The creamy white cliffs of the Seven Sisters, overlooking the
English Channel at the end of the path, are in striking contrast
to the suburban surroundings of south London, where the
Vanguard Way starts. It is indeed a novel idea to begin a walk
outside a railway station in East Croydon!

Finally, the West Mendip Way (Chapter 12) follows a route
across a range of hills not especially well known but
particularly popular with geologists. There are curiosities at
every turn, notably Cheddar Gorge and Wookey Hole.

The West Mendip Way is the shortest path among the
twelve; Glyndwr's Way at 120 miles (192 km) is the longest.
Amounting to nearly 800 miles (1,280 km) in all, the distances do
vary, but to make the routes seem slightly less awesome I have
divided each walk into sections of between 6 and 30 miles (10
and 48 km). With one or two exceptions, the distances covered
in these sections on average represent a day's walking.
Everyone has their own way of tackling a long-distance path,
of course. Some tend to hurry; others prefer a more leisurely
pace. How many miles to aim for in a day is part of the
planning of the walk.

Accommodation is generally easy to come by. In some
instances, it may be necessary to travel several miles from the
actual route to find an inn or guesthouse, and in the peak
season, it is advisable to book in advance. If this type of

accommodation is not your preference, there are a number of youth hostels and camp sites to be found on or near the route of the path.

I never took a tent with me on these walks, opting instead for the comparative luxury of bed and breakfast accommodation, and I always managed to reach my destination by nightfall – albeit with a bit of a rush on some occasions! Some of the routes are tough and quite demanding in places and really should be attempted only by the more experienced hiker. At the beginning of each walk, I have described briefly the nature of the terrain. In addition to this, I have included details of the relevant Landranger and Outdoor Leisure Ordnance Survey Maps. As some form of written guide exists for each of the paths, I have added a bibliography section, indicating where the appropriate publication can be obtained. It is most important that you arm yourself with maps and a copy of the guide relating to each specific route. I have described these paths only in very general terms; precise and detailed notes on route-finding are not included.

I realize that in time some publications may be difficult to come by. Although there is the inter-library loan scheme, I would recommend that you first seek the help of the Long Distance Paths Advisory Service (LDPAS). The Service gives up-to-date information by collating data on the 400-plus named routes throughout the country and on the accompanying books and leaflets available. The database is stored on its own computer system and the scale and variety of the information are enormous. They include details of each path, together with data relating to maps, transport, where a path starts and finishes, how difficult or easy it is and whether it coincides with other routes during its course. The LDPAS receives a grant from the Countryside Commission but operates as an independent body.

Please remember that all our footpaths are, of course, subject to change; minor rerouting and revised or improved way-marking are among the most common occurrences. As I write this introduction I am reminded that a proposal to extend the Speyside walk as far as Banff on the Moray coast is at present under consideration, while Glyndwr's Way is being considered for adoption by the Countryside Commission and is currently the subject of a feasibility study.

I am sure I will be accused of bias, but I can genuinely say that I enjoyed all the walks immensely, though being a keen hill walker I make no secret of the fact that Scotland and the north of England are where I am most at home. To me these walks are much more than just a lengthy tramp in the countryside. They are uniquely intimate experiences which give a fascinating insight into the heart and soul of rural Britain. Every precious ingredient of our varied and ever-changing landscape is here.

Walking these routes, it is very difficult not to strike up conversations with locals and end up swapping stories with fellow hikers. I know I am at my happiest after perhaps a day's marching in the wind and rain, relaxing over a drink or two beside a log fire in a friendly inn and reflecting on the memorable events of the day. It must be the masochistic streak in me, but in my opinion the last few hundred yards are the best bit of the whole adventure. The sense of achievement that comes with the final leg of the walk is surely unique. You may look bedraggled and physically exhausted after the rigours of the previous few days, but that singular feeling of accomplishment at the end makes the whole exercise worthwhile.

Finally, if it does nothing else, I hope this guide will inspire you to leave the comfort and safety of your armchair and head for the hills and the wide-open spaces. That is surely the only way to appreciate and experience at first hand our wonderful rural heritage. I do not believe that any of you will regret it.

The publisher and author would like to thank all those who helped supply photographs for this book, and also Nicola Wastie for her illustrations.

1 The Two Moors Way

The Two Moors Way was established by the RA but there were times when the whole project was in serious danger of being abandoned altogether. If it hadn't been for sheer determination and a good deal of pioneering spirit, doubtless there would have been no path now.

The original idea was for a national long-distance footpath with the backing of the Countryside Commission, but this was eventually dropped, mainly because of legal difficulties, lack of political will and, more significantly, strong opposition from local landowners. However, after lengthy negotiations the route was revised and, by keeping to existing rights of way and minor roads, at last, in May 1976, a Royal Marine helicopter carried a tiny handful of people across the route of the walk for the official opening ceremony of the Two Moors Way. Four granite plaques at Ivybridge, Drewsteignton, Morchard Bishop and Lynmouth commemorate the occasion.

Cleverly, the path is a fine link between two of Britain's most popular national parks, Dartmoor and Exmoor, the latter being the smallest of all of them and somehow less hostile. Dartmoor is sometimes a cruel, featureless landscape, uncompromisingly cold and inhospitable in places. Exmoor, on the other hand, is softer and altogether more welcoming. But the path is not all moorland walking. Away from the wild expanses, there are excursions into unspoilt, wooded river valleys and along peaceful stretches of river bank which provide a welcome alternative to the open, exposed country.

Beginning at Ivybridge in South Devon, the way climbs to Ugborough Moor, passing en route the remains of various Bronze Age settlements. North of the village of Widecombe-in-the-Moor, with its dominant church tower distantly visible, its throngs of curious visitors and its deliciously sinister tale of dark mystery, the way follows Dartmoor paths and uninvaded tracts of land through more villages, Chagford and Drewsteignton, with their fine historic buildings and snug cottages.

Length 103 miles (164 km)
Start Ivybridge
Finish Lynmouth
Going Quite a few easy stretches, but some hard stages over higher exposed ground
Ordnance Survey Maps 180, 181, 191, 202
Outdoor Leisure Map 28 – Dartmoor
Waymarking Commemorative stones, waymarker posts and arrows; a compass is essential in poor weather as some stages of the route are undefined

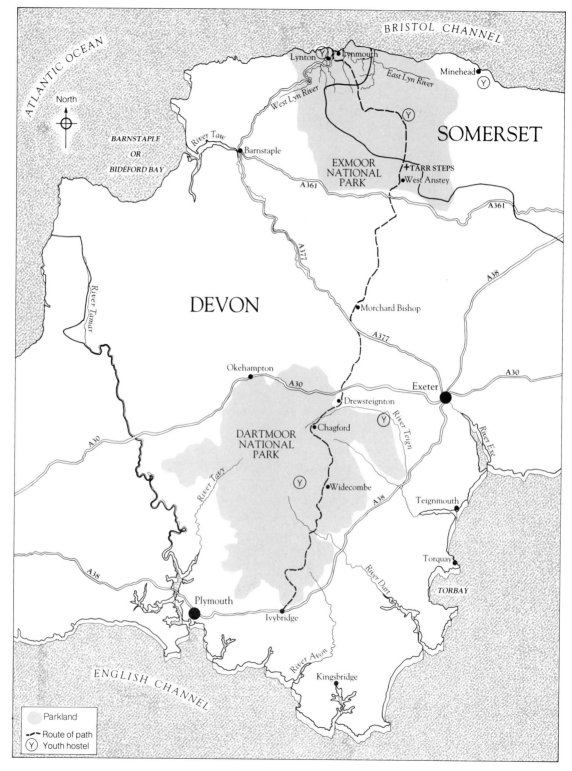

Beyond the national park boundary the route crosses the farmland of mid-Devon, through Morchard Bishop, Witheridge and Knowstone, before entering the Exmoor National Park, near the famous beauty spot of Tarr Steps, surely on the itinerary of every West Country visitor.

The final leg beyond Withypool is over open moorland once again and through lovely Exmoor valleys barely touched by time – the hidden romantic landscape of R. D. Blackmore's *Lorna Doone*. The approach into Lynmouth on the north Devon coast is steep but spectacular. The pretty village suffers from commercial overkill, though it is easy to understand why the likes of Shelley, Wordsworth and Coleridge loved it so.

Finally, take care. Much of the route is hilly and can be very wet and muddy in places, so good boots and plenty of protective clothing are essential.

Accommodation is generally available in many of the towns and villages along the route. Buses and coaches serve the towns at the start and finish of the walk. There are trains to Plymouth near the start and from Taunton near the finish.

Ivybridge to Widecombe-in-the-Moor
20 miles (32 km)

The River Erme flows picturesquely through the centre of this pleasant town with its assortment of brightly coloured houses, cottages and inns, located at the extreme southern edge of Dartmoor. The river is perhaps its most notable feature; other

One of four inscribed granite plaques located at intervals along the route of the Two Moors Way. This one is on the northern outskirts of Ivybridge.

than that it is pretty unremarkable, apart from the old paper mill situated on the sharp bend in the road as it makes for Harford.

The way leaves Ivybridge by heading north and passing the first of the commemorative stones denoting the date of the path's official opening. Crossing the main Western Region railway line, with its 125 trains sliding almost effortlessly over the track below, the route follows a quiet country road up towards Stowford House, where the Royal Agricultural Society of England is to be found. There are good views along this stretch over woodland and back towards Ivybridge.

Soon the way leaves the road and quickly makes for wild, hostile moorland in the vicinity of the old Red Lake tramway. The now-disused track was constructed in 1910 to accommodate the Red Lake china clay works. From the track there are splendid views in fine weather along the Channel coast towards Plymouth and Cornwall. Along this section, too, there are many prehistoric monuments, enclosures and cairns, as well as a curious 2-mile-long (3-km) stone row. Beginning at a stone circle and extending to a cairn on Green Hill, it is the longest stone row on Dartmoor.

North again over the Moor to a spot known as Crossways (beyond it is the site of the old Red Lake workings, where Canada geese have been known to raise their young). Red Lake pool is a favourite meeting place for Dartmoor ponies. Most of the time they are left to their own devices but once a year the young animals are rounded up and herded off to be sold at market. Traditionally, Dartmoor ponies have long been a popular feature in these parts. Holiday-makers, children and local people regard the gentle creatures fondly.

Further north the way crosses the granite clapper bridge over the River Avon and then stumbles upon the Huntingdon Cross, thought to have been here as early as the sixteenth century. Just near it on the north bank of the river lie the ruins of tiny Keeble Martin's Church, built in 1909 and named after the celebrated botanist and painter who interestingly was also a clergyman.

Soon the path drops down between boulders to cross another river – this time the Mardle – via a wooden footbridge. Now the route is a clear track which widens to a lane leading to the little village of Scorriton. Note the good views away to the right towards Torbay and its colourful seaside resorts of Torquay and Paignton. Scorriton is a sleepy little community with a charming collection of houses and cottages and, all-important for walkers, the Tradesman's Arms in the centre of the village.

Scorriton's neighbour is the larger village of Holne, where the vicarage was the birthplace in 1819 of the writer Charles Kingsley. Holne is a most attractive place with impressive

Opposite Ivybridge on Dartmoor's southern boundary. The rock-strewn River Erme winds between the trees. In the thirteenth century the bridge was wide enough to accommodate only a single packhorse. However, Plymouth's subsequent prosperity gave it greater status.

New Bridge spanning the River Dart. The river and the overhanging trees make this a perfect spot. The narrow bridge is hardly new; quite possibly, it is the oldest road bridge on Dartmoor.

views of the river valley and several historic buildings of some note. The Church of St Mary dates to the fourteenth century and has a painted medieval screen. Next to it is the Church House Inn, with its imposing entrance overlooking the street. It was built incredibly in 1329. Just along the street is the Old Forge tearoom, for those who cannot resist scrumptious Devon cream teas. There are tables outside and indoors you can purchase postcards and souvenirs.

North of Holne, the path descends to Cleave Wood on the eastern bank of the Dart and follows a glorious stretch of the river between the trees.

New Bridge is to be found deep in this wooded valley. Being by the road, it is a popular picnic spot for locals and holiday-makers alike and is therefore somewhat commercialized. The walks beside the river and through the woods are a delight, however. The bridge itself is anything but new. In

fact, it probably dates from the fifteenth century and is new in
the sense that it replaced a previous structure – if anything, it
could be the oldest road bridge on Dartmoor. Its grey arches
and buttresses make it quite distinctive and its handsome design
is greatly enhanced by the wooded setting in which it lies.
Beyond New Bridge the route climbs to Leigh Tor and follows
what is known as Dr Blackall's Drive. Blackall was a local
nineteenth-century squire and this was his carriage drive. The
choice is hardly surprising, for the views from here are
splendid.

Over the road the way heads across open moorland, at
length reaching the village of Ponsworthy. The place has a
soothing air of calm about it, typical of many Dartmoor
villages, and its picturesque thatch and granite cottages have
plenty of charm and character. There is a busy stream flowing
here and a shallow ford beside which the route passes on its
way to Jordan. One of the cottages by the ford was once the
village smithy.

Jordan is a rather remote settlement to the north of
Ponsworthy. At this point the path crosses another river, the

The 120-feet-high (36-m) tower of
St Pancras Church, Widecombe-
in-the-Moor, described as one of
the finest in the west of England.

Opposite Bennett's Cross, Headland Warren. A granite roadside landmark and one of a number of crosses to be found on Dartmoor, either marking medieval boundaries or acting as guide posts for travellers.

West Webburn, by means of a wooden footbridge. Follow the road now towards Widecombe-in-the-Moor.

The fourteenth-century Church of St Pancras, sometimes referred to as the 'Cathedral of the Moors', stands out for miles around. Its tall granite tower dominates the buildings below but is overshadowed itself by the tors of Dartmoor above, in particular Chinkwell Tor. It is a bustling village, packed in summer, more often than not, with visitors and sightseers. There are the familiar rows of cars and coaches and, not surprisingly, the usual tourist facilities.

Near the Church is a quaint square, once the setting for archery practice, which is overlooked by the sixteenth-century Church House, now in the care of the National Trust. Once an almshouse, part of this building is now the village hall.

Widecombe is probably most famous for the song 'Widecombe Fair', about Uncle Tom Cobbleigh and all, but there is a darker, more malevolent side to the village of which few people are aware. It concerns the church and an incident there in 1638. In the middle of a Sunday service, while a violent thunderstorm raged outside, a bolt of fire suddenly hit the church, demolishing a tower pinnacle, killing four people in the congregation and injuring more than sixty more, mainly as a result of burning. The story suggests that one of the survivors recalled seeing a mysterious stranger in the church dressed in black with a cloven hoof. This inevitably fuelled speculation that the thunderbolt was the work of the Devil, who had been seen earlier that day at nearby Poundsgate, a darkly dressed figure breathing fire and apparently riding a black horse.

Widecombe-in-the-Moor to Drewsteignton
19 miles (30 km)

Returning to the walk, follow the ridge of Hamel Down as it climbs to 1,700 feet (515 m), the highest point of the Two Moors Way. Keep to the ridge, deep in heather, for over a mile, noting the grim outline of Princetown and its prison in the far distance. The bleak surroundings lend an even greater air of harsh severity to the prison buildings. Princetown seems somehow to belong in this setting.

Hamel Down is the traditional stamping ground of red grouse in spring and summer. Several thousand years ago inhabitants from the surrounding settlements came here to bury their dead in Bronze Age barrows. Their remains were interred beneath stone slabs and during the last century a grooved dagger and an amber pommel were unearthed when one of the barrows was excavated. The finds were subsequently destroyed, however, during an air raid on Plymouth in the last war. Beyond Hamel Down Tor the way reaches Grimspound,

the remnants of a Bronze Age community that has remained in an excellent state of preservation over the centuries.

From Hookney Tor the path descends to a minor road and then heads west to Bennett's Cross, round the slopes of Birch Tor. This was a tin mining area, with an intricate network of shafts and mine workings, 100 years ago. The remains of buildings and wheelpits can still be seen today, but they no longer scar the Dartmoor landscape in the way that they once did. Over 100 men were employed here and the mines were worked until the early part of this century.

Yet another stone monument, Bennett's Cross, lies beside the B3212 road, a popular route for tourists and holiday-makers, who stop in one of the many car parks or lay-bys to sample the moorland air or simply to admire the vast, uninterrupted views across Dartmoor. Bennett's Cross is probably thirteenth century in date. Originally a guide post for the track between Tavistock and Chagford, it also serves as the northern boundary post for Headland Warren and is a well-known local landmark, frequently to be found on tourist maps and the like and often the subject of drawings and postcards.

Sheep may stray into your path here and if you are dogged by thoughts of rest and refreshment, the isolated Warren House Inn is a short walk along the road heading south-west towards Princetown.

The way aims now for Chagford Common, with its thick carpet of heather and distinctive ancient monuments. Among them is a double stone row nearly 500 feet (152 m) in length and with a cairn at one end. Hut circles can be found nearby also. This is wild, unfriendly territory without clear tracks or way-marks and a compass is vital on this particular stretch.

Crossing Chagford Common, the path joins the Mariners' Way to pass through Yardworthy, with its medieval farmhouse and porch of huge granite blocks, and then goes on to the tiny hamlet of Teigncombe. There the route turns and heads north-east along the Teign Valley to Chagford, following a lane that runs roughly parallel with the River Teign.

Chagford – the name is Old English for a ford in gorse-covered country – is a picturesque village that thrives as a tourist centre for this part of Dartmoor. It is also particularly popular as a base for walking expeditions and tours of Dartmoor's antiquities. Situated on the Teign, Chagford was a stannary town until the middle part of the eighteenth century. Tin, of which there was plenty on the moors at one time, was brought to Chagford and to three other towns in the locality to be assessed and taxed. Should you be contemplating an overnight stop in the village, then The Three Crowns must be considered. The thirteenth-century hotel is reported to be haunted by the poet Sidney Godolphin, who was shot in the porch here by Cromwell's men during the Civil War. A shooting in the nearby churchyard of the fifteenth-century granite church of St Michael is said to have given R. D. Blackmore the inspiration for the wounding of Lorna by her father in his famous novel *Lorna Doone*.

Chagford has many fine houses and buildings and is perhaps most attractive around the bustling village square and main street. The octagonal Market House is mid-nineteenth century in date and replaces a previous building.

From the village, the Two Moors Way follows the north bank of the Teign to the narrow, hump-backed seventeenth-century Rushford Bridge. Beyond it the path crosses the A832 road at Dogmarsh Bridge.

Continuing along the river bank and over a small stream by means of stepping stones, the path suddenly swings left and up towards the granite edifice of Castle Drogo. The route follows the Hunter's Path as it cuts through the trees and between steep slopes of bracken, with the walls of the castle visible above. At a height of over 900 feet (273 m), Castle Drogo commands a superb position above the river valley and affords glorious views over unspoilt Devon countryside and moorland. Owned by the National Trust, it is a cunning fake, completed only this century. Designed by Sir Edwin Lutyens for Julius Drewe of

The modern medieval lines of Castle Drogo. One of Lutyens's masterpieces, England's newest castle was built this century for Julius Drewe, who established the Home and Colonial Stores grocery chain. Drewe died in 1931 and Castle Drogo was presented to the National Trust by his grandson in 1974.

Chagford High Street. The Three Crowns Hotel on the left is one of Chagford's most notable buildings. In 1643 it witnessed a skirmish between Royalist forces and Cromwell's soldiers, who were using the inn as a billet.

Home and Colonial Stores fame, it was finished in 1930, a year before Drewe's death. Of modern medieval design, it is generally regarded as one of Lutyens's finest works and a visit to Castle Drogo also affords the opportunity to inspect its gardens: acres of elegantly landscaped grounds as well as an enormous circular lawn enclosed by a yew hedge. Access is by a signposted path via Sharp Tor, further along the Hunter's Path.

Returning to the walk, turn left just beyond Sharp Tor and

leave the high-level path with its views over the wooded gorge and the river, heading now for the village of Drewsteignton.

The square tends to dominate Drewsteignton, with its gathering of cob and thatch cottages and the picturesque Drewe Arms guarding the entrance to the fifteenth-century church of Holy Trinity. A plaque at the gate reveals that the little church cottage beside the entrance was purchased by public subscription and given to the church for use of the caretaker in grateful memory of the life of William Ponsford, a churchwarden in this parish between 1901 and 1931.

Drewsteignton to Morchard Bishop
15 miles (24 km)

From the village, the path heads north down to Veet Mill and over a stream by a small wooden bridge. The way now follows a lane to Winscombe, where it crosses the A30 by means of an overpass.

The Drewe Arms, Drewsteignton. The Drewe name still exerts its influence. The thatched inn is early eighteenth century in date and overlooks a square of picturesque cottages. The perfectly shaped village is a conservation area and stands on the crest of a ridge.

The dual carriageway marks the northern boundary of the Dartmoor National Park and the route ahead is to Exmoor, over pleasant, gently rolling farmland – softer and less spectacular than the scenery of Dartmoor, but typically West Country in character, with its high hedgerows and deep-red soil.

Passing the parish church of St Andrew at Hittisleigh, the way follows the road for some time. Take the road to Newby Farm and then cross yet another river, the Troney. In about a mile the path reaches West Wotton and then joins the road again for a short spell.

Beyond the Exeter–Okehampton railway line, the way follows the route of Webber Lane, an old drovers' track, and adjacent to it the delightful woodland of Waterford Plantation plays host to the long-tailed tit and the goldcrest, among other birds preferring the conifer trees for nesting.

Joining the road at Whelmstone Cross, the path continues north, passing Whelmstone Barton. The present house dates from the beginning of the seventeenth century. Once the manor house, Whelmstone Barton is a delightful blend of cob, thatch and brick chimney stacks.

Clannaborough – the name means 'cloven hill' – is the next stop on the Two Moors Way. A tiny place, it is not really a village at all, but it does boast a small church dedicated to the Celtic St Petrock. The rectory is thatched, with a wood-pillared porch.

Crossing the A3072, the route makes for Lammacott Farm and then goes across country to reach the A377 near Wolfin Farm. Hikers should take care at this stage as the route follows the busy main road for a short distance, going briefly along a footpath on the grass verge.

Leaving the road, the route heads for Peter's Green, drops down to a small stream and then climbs towards the church at Morchard Bishop – a village with a delightfully rural West Country ring to its name. Standing quietly on a hill, it can provide refreshment and overnight accommodation. There are good views over towards Dartmoor and Exmoor from the fifteenth-century parish church of St Mary's, where a copper beech tree stands in the corner of the churchyard.

Morchard Bishop to Withypool
30 miles (48 km)

From Morchard Bishop, the path heads across country to Beech Hill, where colonies of rooks make their nests in the trees. The route is again over undulating farmland, through woodland. At length it reaches Washford Pyne and just through this tiny hamlet it crosses the River Dalch.

The next section provides glimpses of Witheridge church as

the path cuts across fields and farm tracks on its way to this village, set in the valley of the Little Dart River. Witheridge is a conservation area and includes many fine eighteenth- and nineteenth-century buildings of plastered rubble and cob, brick chimney stacks and a smattering of thatched roofs – all traditional ingredients for this part of the West Country. Mentioned in the Domesday Book, Witheridge had a medieval weekly market and a midsummer fair to celebrate the dedication of the parish church of St John the Baptist, which was restored in 1876.

From the village, drop down across field paths to the charmingly named Little Dart River and follow the southern bank heading east through the trees. Quite soon the route joins a country road and just the other side of Bradford Bridge, it passes Bradford Barton, a charming old farmhouse probably dating back to the eighteenth century and originally a Domesday Manor.

This next section is essentially high ground, with grand, sweeping views extending south to Dartmoor and northwards to the pretty moorland country around the villages of Knowstone and Rackenford. The roads here are delightfully quiet and traffic-free and the beech hedgerows give shield and protection to a veritable treasure trove of wild flowers and plants. One story goes that ramblers passing this way have been able to stop for a blackberry snack even at the height of autumn.

Keep on the road until reaching a field just before the village centre at Knowstone. This leads to the churchyard of the medieval church of St Peter, beyond which is the narrow main street with its charming houses and cottages. The village has been scheduled a conservation area and the thirteenth-century Masons Arms is ideal for rest and refreshment.

From the village, the way follows a 'No through road' to Owlaborough Farm and then out towards the open expanse of Owlaborough Moor, where soaring buzzards may frequently be seen, their dark, menacing shapes somehow adding a sinister air of mystery to the landscape.

The way crosses the A361 road further on and by the Jubilee Inn takes the road to Yeo Mill. This is followed by a further stretch of road for about a mile until just beyond Wychwood. Then follow the path north until it joins the road at West Anstey. The village has the usual complement of colour-washed cottages. Nearby is the church of St Petrock.

Keep to the road as far as the junction at Badlake Moor Cross, the southern boundary of the Exmoor National Park, and then take the track north, with open moorland scenery over on the left. Passing the Benford Stone – originally one of a line signifying the course of an old boundary – the path tramps on over the moors towards Hawkridge.

On the road again the way passes two landmarks of some note. First, there is Slade Bridge, below which the Dane's Brook runs, marking the Devon and Somerset border. Then, just beyond it, is Slade Barn, a sturdy, ancient stone building with a hay store and shelter for animals below it. A stone's throw away, across a field, is the road into Hawkridge. Take it and enter the village. There is accommodation here and a twelfth-century church which should be visited.

The next 2 miles (3 km) of the Two Moors Way offer some of the prettiest scenery in the entire journey – not the wild, spectacular landscapes of moorland and hill, but picturesque, low-lying river valley and woodland as at last the route encounters the banks of the River Barle.

First, the path runs alongside the beech and ash trees of Great Cleave to reach Parsonage Farm, on the far side of Row Down Wood. The way turns east here and makes for Tarr Steps, a multiple clapper bridge over the Barle and one of Exmoor's most famous and intriguing landmarks. In spite of its remote setting, buried by trees at the foot of a winding country lane, or perhaps because of it, Tarr Steps are a major attraction with visitors, though thankfully, because of worries over traffic congestion, the unsightly car park and toilet facilities are hidden from view about 900 feet (273 m) further up the road.

The Steps have seventeen spans but no one is quite sure where the huge stone slabs originally came from. Twice this century the bridge has had to be rebuilt. The last time, in 1952, some of the slabs were washed downstream by the disastrous flood of that year. Its exact age is unknown, but it is believed to be medieval. Certainly there is a strong sense of history here and somehow an air of mystery about it, too, that cannot be dispelled by the flocks of visitors who come here to gaze at it and photograph it.

The route to Withypool is along the banks of the River Barle, through peaceful meadows and woodland. Whatever the weather, but especially when the sun is shining, the river looks enchanting, its sparkling waters dancing between the trees. It is a lovely hidden corner of the National Park, away from the well-used tourist trails and the crowds, although walkers and fishermen favour it and, after all, it is there for public enjoyment and should be seen and admired. The odd red deer or otter may come into view, but not that often. If they do, then their presence will surely enhance your journey.

If the river is high between Tarr Steps and Withypool, then there is an alternative route up over Withypool Hill. Withypool itself is a pleasant place for a stop. The seventeenth-century Royal Oak Inn does bed and breakfast if you need to break your journey here. The Exford Youth Hostel is a short walk from the village.

Opposite Tarr Steps. Hidden delightfully among trees away from Exmoor's moorland expanses, this famous antiquity draws many visitors. Spanning the River Barle, the clapper bridge has been rebuilt several times due to serious flooding.

Exmoor's rounded hills and combes from Blue Gate. Exmoor is Britain's smallest national park but there is a wide variety of landscape within its 265 square miles (686 sq km). Soft, swelling moorland, heather-clad commons and wooded ravines form an integral part of the scenery.

Withypool to Lynmouth
19 miles (30 km)

Begin this final stretch by taking the 'No through road' behind the village shop and post office and then following a way-marked path across farmland. The way keeps to the road for a while before crossing the Barle beyond Horsen Farm and just below Cow Castle. This prominent landmark was once an Iron Age hillfort, covering almost 3 acres (7 ha).

Cornham Ford occupies a delightful setting enclosed by quiet hills and moorland and it is here yet again that the path crosses the river. Dippers are quite a common sight, their heads suddenly ducking beneath the water in their quest for a tasty morsel or two on the river bed.

This next stage marks the highest point on the Exmoor section of the Two Moors Way as the route follows open fields and moorland straddling the B3558 near Simonsbath, a pretty village beside the River Barle.

Pushing on, the path reaches the Hoar Oak Valley and then the Hoar Oak tree. This landmark signifies the ancient Royal Forest boundary. A tree has always stood on this spot, but whereas up until the beginning of the nineteenth century this was hunting ground, nowadays much of the land here is given over to grazing.

The home stretch to Lynton and Lynmouth begins by following Cheriton Ridge between the valleys of the Hoar Oak Water and the Farley Water, stumbling upon more ancient monuments here and there.

More interestingly, perhaps, this is Lorna Doone country, though this whole area seemed to provide Blackmore with a rich and endless source of inspiration for his classic novel. Over to the right lies Brendon Common and Badgworthy Water, and Hoccombe Combe between the two is reputed to be where the famous outlaws in the story lived.

Beyond Cheriton the path heads for Hillsford Bridge, following a route alongside the river. Continue along the A39 for a short distance and then take the path signposted to Lynmouth. The way passes a turning to Watersmeet. Having almost completed the entire 100 miles (160 km) of the walk by now, a short diversion here will make little or no difference to your physical state. It is certainly worthwhile. Watersmeet, as its name so enchantingly implies, is where the East Lyn River and the Hoar Oak Water unite in a spectacular wooded gorge, where the rushing river and the road can be glimpsed running parallel far below. Autumn is the best time to see this deep ravine, when the leaves are a deep, rich blend of brown, orange and gold. Then it cannot fail to impress.

Returning to the Two Moors Way, the path zigzags across Myrtleberry Cleave, beneath which lies Lynmouth and the Channel. Access to the Lynbridge Youth Hostel is near Oxen Tor, where the path heads for Summer House Hill. The main path continues over Lyn Cleave and drops with formidable steepness into the village of Lynmouth, where the walk ends opposite the car park in the main street.

Lynmouth and Lynton sound almost like a music-hall double act. Instead, they are two picturesque villages, one almost vertically above the other. They are typically West Country in the look of their whitewashed thatched cottages, perching so precariously on the thickly wooded cliffs. Lynmouth is the lower of the two. The harbour, where the East and West Lyn rivers flow into Lynmouth Bay, is a delight. However, it was a very different picture in the summer of 1952, when a sudden storm hit the area and the Lyn, already swollen from weeks of heavy rain, at last broke its banks and raged through Lynmouth, devouring every object and every living creature in

its path. The village was devastated and thirty-four people perished. About 90 million gallons of water washed down on the village that night and it was years before Lynmouth's familiar sense of calm was restored. Nowadays, thanks to civil engineering, even in full spate the river runs safely through Lynmouth and out to sea.

The charm of Lynmouth has impressed not only holiday-makers but also poets and writers over the years. Coleridge fell under its spell and in 1812 Shelley stayed here with his teenage bride, Mary Wollstonecraft, using the place as a secret hideaway where for a while at least they could escape the wrath of her parents.

Lynmouth Harbour, tranquil and picturesque beneath the steep wooded slopes. However, the picture is a far cry from the terrible disaster of 1952, when a cloudburst pushed floodwater downriver into Lynmouth, destroying homes and claiming more than thirty lives in its path.

Opposite River Barle near Simonsbath. The way crosses the Barle by means of a ford.

Other attractions include a splendid Victorian cliff railway up to Lynton, operated by use of a water tank incorporated into each car and provided by Sir George Newnes, the publisher, who had an abiding love of the place. There is also the Valley of Rocks, an extraordinary collection of peaks and outcrops, including Castle Rock, which at 800 feet (242 m) is one of the highest landmarks along Britain's coastline.

Undertaking this walk in mid-summer, you will be glad you were without transport as both Lynton and Lynmouth become absurdly cluttered with cars and visitors, and although they are among Devon's coastal gems, you will soon long for the lofty, unpopulated expanses of Exmoor and Dartmoor once again. Whatever the conditions, however, this is a suitably spectacular setting in which to finish the Two Moors Way.

BIBLIOGRAPHY
The Two Moors Way official guide, with maps, sketches and directions, is available from:
J. R. Turner
Coppins
The Poplars
Pinhoe
Exeter
Devon EX4 9HH

2 The Isle of Wight Coastal Path

The Romans called it Vectis but it was Queen Victoria and Prince Albert who made the Isle of Wight fashionable when they built a holiday home, Osborne House, at Cowes in the middle of the last century. Today there is still that dignified air about it and as a holiday haunt it is just as popular as ever with tourists and visitors.

Being an island it has an identity all of its own. In places its appearance is almost continental and its sheltered position in the Solent gives it a mild climate even in winter.

To complete the entire circuit of the Isle of Wight on foot is really the only way to appreciate the natural beauty and unique variety of its coastal scenery, for there is much to see. Alum Bay is heavily commercialized but there are spectacular views of the cliffs and the famous Needles rocks and lighthouse a mile beyond. Much of the path in the south of the island is a straight, relatively easy walk over high chalk downs and beyond Freshwater Bay the coast is often remote, exposed and largely uninhabited. In between the frequent chines, the cliffs are precipitous and constant coastal erosion has resulted in the path now running very close to the cliff edge in places, so take care.

The graceful period architecture of Ventnor and Shanklin is pleasing to the eye, though the seafront attractions include the ubiquitous amusement arcades. From St Catherine's Point near Ventnor as far as the Regency resort of Ryde the coastline is softer and generally more urban, with a greater concentration of towns and villages, holiday homes and hotel accommodation. Bembridge and Seaview are prime examples.

Cowes, of course, means sailing. It is the undisputed yachting capital of the nation and the height of colourful activity during Cowes week every August. Less well known perhaps are nearby Wootton Bridge, ancient but peaceful Newtown and Yarmouth, all with their moored yachts, boats and winding estuaries.

Length 65 miles (104 km)
A circular route with a suggested start and finish at Yarmouth

Going Easy with several short climbs

Ordnance Survey Map 196

Outdoor Leisure Map 29 – Isle of Wight

Waymarking Blue signposts with white writing are positioned where the direction of the path is not obvious

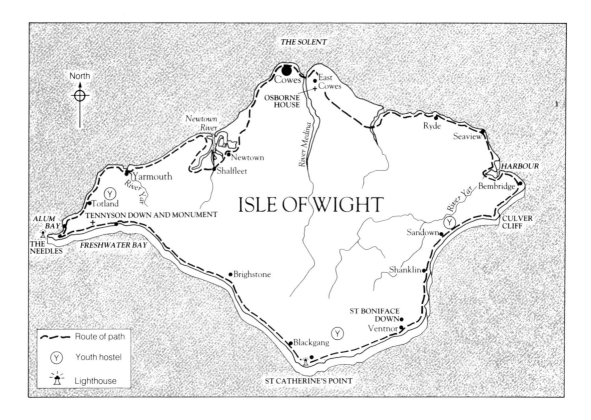

Though there are many hidden bays and quiet stretches of coast, the Isle of Wight is only 23 miles (37 km) long and 13 miles (21 km) wide. During the summer the island's population is greatly increased by holiday-makers, who come over for its long hours of sunshine, its safe bathing and its sandy beaches. The roads are often crammed with cars and coaches, which makes a walk around the coastline a perfect way of exploring the island without too much aggravation. Certain stretches of the route are by road, but mostly it is over cliff-top paths, tracks, sea walls and esplanades. Nearly 40 miles (64 km) of it is beside the coast, but even the inland stretches are never very far from the sea. Being a circular walk, you can begin wherever there is a ferry terminal, though Yarmouth is as good a place as any to start. Accommodation is not normally a problem. There is a wide selection to choose from, even in the less-populated south-west corner of the island.

Yarmouth to Grange
15 miles (24 km)

Yarmouth is a quaint place from which to start the coastal path. With its picturesque square, colourful houses and

cottages, inns and coffee shops, it is a fine introduction to the island as you step off the ferry from Lymington near the town's 600-feet (182-m) Victorian pier. Apart from the buildings, it is noteworthy for the parish church of St James at one end of the square and the Royal Solent Yacht Club at the other. Also worth a look is the castle, dating back to the middle of the sixteenth century. It was built by Henry VIII as a coastal defence against the French, who regarded the Isle of Wight as a convenient stepping stone in their plan to invade Britain.

Leave Yarmouth and its bright, bustling harbour by making for the road bridge over the River Yar. Soon the path heads along the sea wall, with Yarmouth, its church and its forest of masts providing a pretty backdrop. Shortly the views of the Solent are obscured by trees as the path cuts through the Fort Victoria Country Park. The only sound to break the silence is that of birdsong or shipping in the Needles Passage. It was this narrow stretch of the Solent between the island and the mainland that Fort Victoria was built to defend in 1853. What remains of the fort today is in the care of the Isle of Wight County Council and forms part of an attractive 50-acre (124-ha) country park, offering the usual leisure facilities, including picnic areas and nature trails.

Alum Bay is a popular part of the island, due in no small measure to these distinctive multi-coloured cliffs. The coastal path crosses Headon Warren before descending to Alum Bay and from this bracing, heather-covered cliff top the views are magnificent.

When you break cover from the trees, you are on high ground with glimpses of the sea. Then a short walk brings you to the first of a number of permanent holiday sites throughout the island. This one is adjacent to Brambles Chine, overlooking Colwell Bay. When the sea mist hangs low over the coast, the sound of the Needles lighthouse hooter wails eerily along this stretch.

Hikers undertaking a walk along the coastal path on warm summer days are now faced with the rather dubious prospect of walking along the beach between groups of sun-worshipping holiday-makers, who will, no doubt, gaze at you blankly as you pass by them.

Joining the sea wall, the route now passes a modest smattering of seaside attractions beneath the steep cliffs before eventually reaching Totland Bay, with its pier, gift shops, ice-cream kiosks and boat trips to the Needles. The Totland Bay Old Lifeboat House beyond the pier was in use between 1885 and 1924. Note the amusing Totland Tides rhyme on the far wall of the building.

Leave the foreshore by the steep steps behind the Old Lifeboat House and climb up to the road at Totland. Soon you are back on paths again as the route heads for Headon Warren, owned by the National Trust. There are glorious views from here of Totland Bay below, the Needles Passage across to the lighthouse at Hurst Castle and, along the Isle of Wight coastline, the route of the path so far. Headon Warren is an ancient barrow or burial mound built about 3,500 years ago by an agricultural community of the early Bronze Age.

The views of Alum Bay and this corner of West Wight are magnificent as the path descends in zigzag fashion through the heather and ling towards the huge car and coach parks at Alum, rarely deserted on hot summer days. The walk from Headon Warren down to Alum also provides an excellent insight into the nature of the island's landscape and in many ways the hinterland, in places, is almost as dramatic as the coastal scenery. It is rolling farmland, with undisturbed little villages almost buried from view and broad sweeps of downland as far as the eye can see. But it is really the beauty of the island's coastline that appeals so strongly to the visitor.

What you find at Alum Bay will be in sharp contrast to all that has gone before, with its heavy concentration of gift shops, snack bars, cafés, pottery shops, popcorn stands and huge numbers of summer visitors to clog up the place and help keep it prosperous and thriving. There is even a chair lift to the beach and a model railway included in the leisure park. The attractions are all very well for the visiting holiday-maker, but those passing through here on foot will probably be inclined to quicken their pace at the prospect of so much brash commercialism. But before you go, pause for a few moments in the central car park to study the monument – an odd place to find it, but this marks the site of Marconi's first coastal wireless station.

The multi-coloured cliffs at Alum are best seen from the narrow road leading out towards the Needles. The coastal path follows this route, so you are not being taken out of your way. The bay takes its name from the alum mined there as early as the sixteenth century. Locally, you can buy tubes of the sand – a colourful combination of various minerals, including white quartz, red iron oxide and yellow limonite.

The walk up to the Needles is a rewarding one, with spectacular coastal views. Below the cliff there are glimpses of the pebbly beach at Alum and the little jetty from where boat trips are made along the coast. One of the joys of West Wight at the height of summer is pausing on the grassy cliff top above Alum to listen to the high-pitched cries of children playing on the beach below and watch the boats drifting lazily across the bay. This is the island demonstrating one of its best sides.

At the end of the road is The Needles Old Battery, a fort above which is perched a coastguard station. In the ownership of the National Trust now, the fort was built by Lord Palmerston in 1862 in a dramatic setting on the cliffs 250 feet (78 m) above sea level. A 200-feet-long (61-m) passage provides superb close-up views of the Needles Rocks and there is an interesting exhibition relating to the history of the fort.

About 7,000 years ago the Isle of Wight was joined to the mainland by a chalk ridge. Now all that remains of that ridge are the three distinctive 100-feet (30-m) pinnacles that are forever associated with the island and are surely one of its most important tourist attractions. The lighthouse here was built in 1859, replacing one on the cliffs above.

At this point the way changes direction and begins heading east along Tennyson Down, a huge, breezy ridge of chalk and close-cropped grassland rising nearly 500 feet (152 m) above the sea. The Victorian Poet Laureate Alfred Lord Tennyson lived nearby at Faringford House, now a hotel, and the 38-feet (11-m) monument on the summit of the down is dedicated to his memory, replacing an old beacon which was used as a navigational seamark. In fact, the granite cross overlooks a part of the island Tennyson loved dearly and he spent many happy hours walking these downs almost every day. He claimed that the air here was worth 'sixpence a pint'. With a little imagination it is possible to picture the poet strolling along these cliffs as part of his daily constitutional.

Little has changed here since then. Even the plants and birds are much the same. Look out for cowslips, ragwort and several species of orchid growing on the downs. Cormorants and guillemots are among the birds that nest in the cliffs.

Freshwater Bay is a small resort sheltering beneath the cliffs of Tennyson Down in a horseshoe cove. Dwarfed by the great

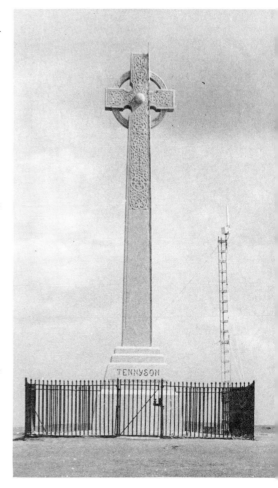

Tennyson Memorial Cross. Tennyson Down is a smooth, whale-backed chalk ridge and here the nineteenth-century Poet Laureate took a rejuvenating stroll every day. When it is clear you can see as far as Portland Bill in the west and Southampton Water across the Solent to the east.

The Needles – Mariners' Milestone. Unquestionably, this is one of the island's most famous and spectacular landmarks. However, strong tidal currents and cross-winds can make this line of serrated, white-tipped rocks a navigational nightmare.

white walls around it, the bay stands undefended against the elements of the sea. Just inland is the source of the River Yar, flowing more or less due north to Yarmouth. After Freshwater Bay the route passes near the golf course on Afton Down and beside a simple stone monument recalling the tragic fate of a fifteen-year-old boy, who fell to his death from the cliffs here in August 1846. Now the path is over rolling grassy cliff tops that are quite rugged and unexplored. This particular stretch, as

far as Blackgang Chine, is probably wilder and more remote than any other part of the island's coast. Cattle graze here and only occasionally is there any sign of civilization to intrude on what is otherwise a rather bleak and barren landscape.

At Shippard's Chine the views inland are of a large, very imposing country house over towards the horizon. This was once the home of the writer J. B. Priestley. As you head eastwards you are never far from the military road, otherwise the A3055, running parallel with the path. The road was built in the 1860s to facilitate troop transportation when the island's coastal defences were strengthened as a precaution against the possibility of French invasion. It eventually became a public road before the Second World War.

Sea vista from Whale Chine. Overlooking Chale Bay the 2-mile (3-km) stretch of beach is one of the least well-known parts of the island.

Grange to Sandown
16 miles (26 km)

About a mile inland from the hamlet of Grange is one of the island's prettiest villages, Brighstone. There are a number of picturesque cottages to see here, as well as accommodation and the opportunity for refreshment, and there is more to the name of the local inn than meets the eye. The Three Bishops is so called because of the three rectors of the parish church, St Mary's, who later became bishops of Bath and Wells, Oxford and Winchester and Salisbury – a proud achievement for a small, quiet community such as this, and one that is commemorated by the marble memorial in the church. French brandy from Cherbourg was the main contraband to come ashore here when smuggling was rife in the area.

Beyond Brighstone the path is a lengthy cliff-top walk with spectacular views in all directions. Skirting Shepherd's Chine – not to be confused with Shippard's Chine – the way reaches Atherfield Point, once notorious for shipwrecks.

Whale Chine is next, followed by a short detour to Chale village, where there is another inn. The churchyard of St Andrew's contains a tomb to those who lost their lives off this coast in 1836, when the 345-ton *Clarendon* was driven ashore and wrecked during a violent storm. This coastline, of course, has always been a danger to shipping and was much used by wreckers.

A narrow path takes you from Chale to Blackgang, which, as visitors are told, was once the haunt of smugglers and wreckers, too, but now enjoys commercial success of a different kind from twentieth-century tourism. As with Alum, Blackgang is invariably saturated with people who come to visit its cliff-top fantasy theme park. There are plenty of exhibitions and reconstructions to see here, but if none of this is to your liking you will want to pass swiftly on and back to the inviting peace and quiet of the cliffs above. From the top there are marvellous views down to the lighthouse at St Catherine's Point and the lush vegetation of the undercliff. Here the land has shifted position to form a verdant, two-tier arrangement of upper and lower cliffs, which are favourite haunts of butterflies. Watch out for the Glanville Fritillary. Named after an eighteenth-century collector, it usually rests on grassy slopes with its wings open. The lighthouse, 136 feet (41 m) above the sea, was built in 1838 as a result of the *Clarendon* tragedy and is the most southerly part of the island.

Gradually the path drops down to St Lawrence, with its prim avenues of Victorian villas. St Lawrence Old Church, now one of the smallest churches in the country, was probably *the* smallest until extended in the 1840s. South of St Lawrence peaceful little Woody Bay lies hidden and undiscovered,

adjacent to the route of the path. A mile or so beyond it, the way brings you into Ventnor's Botanic Gardens, with its smuggling museum. There is a lot to commend Ventnor: its climate, its exuberant architecture and its rocky terraces zigzagging down to the sea. Sheltered by St Boniface Down, nearly 800 feet (242 m) above it, Ventnor's reputation as a winter holiday and health resort is widely known.

The route of the path passes along the seafront, which is quite small, with a sandy beach and the omnipresent amusement arcade. Beyond Ventnor the route is particularly pleasant, taking you through quiet residential roads on the outskirts of the town and then on to Bonchurch. With its pond and rows of cottages, the village is set prettily amidst the trees.

Winterbourne Hotel is buried deep down a lane, away from Bonchurch. For a few months in 1849 it was rented by Charles Dickens and he is said to have written six chapters of *David Copperfield* here. The adjoining church, St Boniface, is a delight, with its flower-filled churchyard and sheltered setting beside the coast. Inside, the ancient church is tiny, almost primitive, with chairs instead of pews. It is only 48 feet (14 m) long by 12 feet (4 m) wide and has the appearance of a private

St Boniface Church. Its setting is charming, nestling among trees and flowers and crumbling gravestones. The sea is visible just a few feet away.

The 6-mile (10-km) arc of Sandown Bay, looking to the south-east corner of the island and over two of its most popular holiday resorts – Shanklin in the foreground and Sandown beyond. In the distance, Culver Cliff glints in the sunshine.

chapel rather than a church. It has an interesting history. Charles I came here from prison at Carisbrooke Castle and Chevalier D'Aux, the French leader, lies buried in an unmarked grave. He was killed when the French raided Bonchurch from the sea in 1545.

From St Boniface the path climbs steeply up into the trees, at times by steps, to what is known as the Landslip, a beautiful wooded, rock-strewn stretch of the coast along which narrow paths wind eastwards under the trees. The paths were originally established by coastguards and customs men who were keeping a secret vigil for smugglers. The Landslip is another example of how the weakness of the ground has gradually changed the area's appearance over the years.

The path then joins the road and descends into Shanklin, giving frequent glimpses of Culver Cliff on the far side of

Sandown Bay. First impressions of Shanklin should be favourable ones. Rylestone Gardens and Shanklin Chine are scenic delights. The Chine is a wooded, flowery glen nearly 300 feet (91 m) deep. A well-loved local beauty spot, it was the scene of bitter conflict with French raiders. It is a peaceful place with a waterfall and a stream cascading through it to a fisherman's cottage, now a pub and restaurant, at the lower end.

Shanklin Old Village has a high street of charming, picture-postcard cottages and the 300-year-old Crab Inn, on the corner as you reach the main road, is a delight. The American poet Henry Longfellow, who stayed nearby in 1868, described the place as: 'the quaintest little village you ever saw. It is all like a scene on a stage.' The fountain in the high street has a verse by Longfellow and the British and American flags adorn the

The charms of Shanklin Old Village – Poets' Corner. This is very much a showpiece, with its lines of quaint thatched cottages and tea shops. Keats stayed in the High Street in 1819 and Longfellow described the village as 'one of the greatest and loveliest places in the Kingdom'.

stonework. Further along there is Keats Green, overlooked by once-fashionable cliff-top hotels. A lift carries passengers down to Shanklin's esplanade, 150 feet (45 m) below the cliff. The pier was partly destroyed by the freak gales of 1987. Shanklin has fine sandy beaches and much period charm, with its Victorian and Edwardian villas and pleasure gardens of hydrangeas. From here it is an easy cliff-top walk to Sandown, about 2 miles (3.2) km) along the coast.

Sandown probably had less appeal than the other resorts and certainly the Victorians never made it as fashionable. Somehow it lacks the zest and vivacity of Ventnor and Shanklin. It is more like a poor relation, though it has the usual holiday attractions, such as gaudy amusement arcades, that now seem to be an accepted part of the holiday scene.

Sandown to Ryde
12 miles (19 km)

The coast path heads east along Sandown's esplanade, passing all the hotels and familiar seaside attractions. Beyond Sandown Zoo and the Yaverland Sailing Boat Club the path climbs up on to Culver Down. Behind you are superb views back across the 6-mile (10-km) golden sweep of Sandown Bay towards Shanklin and Luccombe.

On top of Culver Down, 343 feet (104 m) above the sea, is an imposing monument dedicated to the memory of Charles Anderson Pelham, Earl of Yarborough and First Commodore of the Royal Yacht Squadron. The obelisk is a well-known local landmark and from its position on the cliffs there are fine views over the south-east corner of the island, including Bembridge and St Helens. Looking further north, there are glimpses of Ryde on the opposite coast and Gosport, Portsmouth and Southsea across Spithead.

In the fields below you is Bembridge Airport, where the Islander aircraft is manufactured. The way hugs the coast at Whitecliff Bay through unspoilt scenery and then goes on past Foreland to Bembridge. You then have a choice of beach or adjacent woodland walking as far as Bembridge Harbour.

Bembridge means boats. It thrives on them. The road circling the harbour is lined with boatyards and in the harbour itself there are scores of dilapidated but colourful old houseboats permanently moored alongside the route of the path. Several of them in fact offer bed and breakfast, making a change from the conventional type of holiday accommodation usually to be found on the island. The harbour, a crowded place full of character and spirit, is very much a centre for sailing. There is good bathing at Bembridge. The old Royal Spithead Hotel at the seaward end of the harbour is noteworthy, as is the only remaining windmill on the island, now owned by the National

Trust, which dates from 1700 and is about a mile south-west of the path on the outskirts of the village.

The coastal path skirts the harbour, crosses the River Yar and then cuts back towards the sea beside the remains of an old tidal mill traversing the mill dam by means of a narrow path with the harbour boats now on your right. The way then joins a slender spit known as St Helen's Duver, which protrudes into Bembridge Harbour. The National Trust owns the land, a peaceful haven of grassland, sand dunes and rare flowers where over 200 different species of wild plants have been identified, including sea holly, tree lupin, evening primrose and sea thrift, which transforms large parts of the area into a dazzling splash of pink. Nearby, the ruined tower of St Helen's Church is worth a closer look. Once a priory, all but the tower has been ravaged by the sea over the years.

Union Street, Ryde, with its splendid arcade and preserved shop fronts. The town has a wealth of Regency and Victorian architecture. Ryde pier is visible at the bottom of the street. A regular ferry service to and from the mainland began in 1826.

The way cuts across country for a while to rejoin the coast at Seaview. The name may be rather unimaginative but it is a picturesque place, with a steep street shooting down to the sea and a sandy beach safe for swimming. A plaque on the seafront recalls the fact that in 1545 local militia defeated invading French troops in a bloody battle here. Near it there is a timetable of passing passenger liners, oil tankers and the like to watch out for across Spithead.

The offshore granite forts visible along this stretch of coast are known as 'Palmerston's Follies'. They were built by Lord Palmerston in the 1860s as a coastal defence against possible French invasion. In fact, they were never used.

Seaview to Ryde is flat, easy walking along the sea wall past Puckpool Park, Appley, with its castellated tower and the walls of St Cecilia's Abbey, convent home of the Ryde Sisters.

Soon the holiday attractions of Ryde come into view as the path passes beside the boating lake to join Ryde esplanade. Ryde is a colourful, breezy resort, with a nineteenth-century pier ½ mile (0.8 km) out into the Solent, lines of Victorian and Regency buildings, sandy beaches and the distinctive church spire of All Saints up on the hillside, which is what ferry passengers bound for the island from Portsmouth see long before they spot anything else.

Easy access from the mainland and Queen Victoria's liking for the Isle of Wight made Ryde the island's largest resort and in the holiday season its population can be more than doubled. Two noteworthy attractions are the trains that trundle along the pier – they once served the Piccadilly tube line in London – and Union Street – the steep climb is worth it, if only to visit the delightful Royal Victoria Arcade on the right-hand side.

Ryde to Cowes
7 miles (11 km)

To start off, head towards The Prince Consort, now a pub and coffee house but once the headquarters of the Royal Victoria Yacht Club. Its still-graceful frontage overlooks the sea. The route out of Ryde is a steep one through quiet, residential roads and eventually on to Ryde Golf Links. Binstead Church is enchanting and well worth a look, parts of it dating from Norman times. Its lovely, peaceful setting makes it a must for all visitors to the island.

A short but pleasant walk brings you to Quarr Abbey, founded in 1132 by Cistercian monks. At one time it was used as a defensive blockhouse and a farm. After the Dissolution, however, a new abbey was built ½ mile (0.8 km) away. Just visible through the trees, Quarr Abbey is now the home of Benedictine monks, who lead busy, industrious lives in this

delightful place of worship. The services at the Abbey Church are open to all visitors.

Fishbourne, where there is a Portsmouth car ferry terminal, lies on one side of Wootton Creek, while Wootton village lies on the other. The creek is fringed by pretty woodland and round the corner on the Cowes side there are sandy beaches.

Osborne House – Queen Victoria's 'little paradise'. Prince Albert thought the Solent reminded him of the Bay of Naples, while for Queen Victoria Osborne was a perfect retreat and it was here that she died in 1901.

NICOLA WASTIE

The Prince Consort at Ryde, overlooking the Solent.

A short detour to the south brings you to Firestone Copse at the head of the creek, where it is possible to stroll peacefully among the oaks and hazel trees by the water's edge. The copse is a favourite haunt of bird-watchers and a haven for wild daffodils.

From Wootton Bridge the final leg of this stretch to Cowes is by road at the moment, along either the A3021 or the quieter alternative through Whippingham, a scattered village a little inland from the coast where the legendary yachtsman Uffa Fox went to school.

Osborne House, with its extensive, tree-shaded grounds, is on the right of the A3021 as you approach the outskirts of East Cowes. It is open during the spring, summer and early winter months and is certainly worth a visit if time permits. The house was Queen Victoria's 'little paradise', her island home, and it was here that she died in 1901. Designed jointly in 1845 by her husband, the Prince Consort, and Thomas Cubitt the architect in the style of an Italianate villa, apparently because Prince Albert felt the Solent resembled the Bay of Naples, Osborne was where she could escape from the public glare for a while. It held many happy memories for her and for Albert, and today, mercifully, little has changed at the house, which has remained almost exactly as it was when she lived here (which was on and off, for fifty years). The state apartments can be visited, as can the Swiss Cottage, a life-sized dolls' house, where the Royal children played. Queen Victoria's son Edward VII gave the house to the nation in 1902 and today it is a convalescent home.

Cowes itself has a lot more to offer than East Cowes, which is all Red Funnel Ferries and hovercrafts. The River Medina divides the town and is crossed by means of the floating bridge. Arriving in the town from East Cowes, you are immediately greeted by its quaint, narrow streets, ancient buildings and, between them, glimpses of the harbour and the yacht clubs. Cowes is synonymous with yacht-racing: Cowes week every August is an integral part of the English season and a long-established tradition in the sailing calendar. Now the island's main port, Cowes did not really become a yachting centre until the 1890s, when Edward, Prince of Wales, raced there.

The way passes along the Parade before reaching the headquarters of the Royal Yacht Squadron, overlooking the Solent at the entrance to the harbour. The air of quiet

The great yachting centre of Cowes. The town, divided by the River Medina, is spanned by a floating bridge. Apart from its yacht-racing associations, Cowes provides a ferry and hydrofoil service to and from Southampton.

Cowes Castle – headquarters of the Royal Yacht Squadron. Throughout history the island has been vulnerable to attack and Cowes Castle was built by Henry VIII to defend the Solent. The Royal Yacht Squadron was established in 1815.

superiority as you pass its graceful façade is almost tangible.

If you are undertaking the walk during Cowes week, the scene around you will be anything but dull, with numerous regattas held here during the nine-day event. Other major attractions, such as the Fastnet and Power Boat races, also provide plenty of entertaining activity on this stretch of the Solent.

Cowes to Yarmouth
15 miles (24 km)

The way follows the Parade as it becomes the Prince's Esplanade, opened by the Prince of Wales in 1926. From it there are fine views across to Calshot and Fawley, a short distance away on the Hampshire coast. The unsightly chimneys of Fawley oil refinery push skyward on the horizon.

Beyond Gurnard Bay the coastal path leaves smooth, flat surfaces and follows a grassy cliff-top path as far as Thorness

Bay. The path heads inland here and cuts through holiday camps and farmland before a spell on quiet country roads brings you to the village of Porchfield. Adjacent to it is Newtown, probably the oldest borough on the island and without doubt a village with a most interesting history and background. In the thirteenth and fourteenth centuries Newtown was a thriving port, possibly with greater status than even Newport. But over the years the town fell into decline and all that remains of it today are a few houses and cottages and the Old Town Hall, built in 1699, restored in 1933 and now owned by the National Trust. It is open at certain times of the week between April and September.

The path cuts through the site of the old town and with a little imagination it is possible to identify several of the original streets, laid out in 1256 by the Bishop of Winchester, though

The Town Hall, Newtown. Owned by the National Trust, this ancient brick and stone building is one of the few remaining relics of a once-prosperous port, now a ruined and forgotten place.

much of it is barely recognizable now under a thick carpet of greenery. It is a curious place, belonging firmly in the past – quiet, sad and undiscovered, with its lazy river winding silently towards the sea.

From here it is a short walk to Shalfleet, where there is a chance to pause for refreshment and a well-earned rest at the New Inn. There is, however, another short spell on the road after Shalfleet. Then it is across country again, along paths and tracks heading back in the direction of Newtown River and its estuary, which is a maze of shingle, sand and saltmarsh creeks enclosed within an 800-acre (1977-ha) nature reserve. The entire estuary, which is 14 miles (22 km) in all, together with 4 miles (6 km) of Solent foreshore, is in the care of the National Trust. Sea lavender grows in profusion beside the estuary and the place is a haven, too, for ornithologists, with over 160 different species, including shelducks, red-breasted mergansers, avocets and ospreys, known to visit the island's shores here.

The path swings west at the point where the river meets the sea and follows a winding, tree-shaded path with views of the Solent and Yarmouth Pier. On a hot day the trees and the coastal breeze provide welcome relief from the heat of the sun. It is back to the road again for the last mile as you approach the end of the walk at Yarmouth. At the common, bear right away from the A3054 and walk down between the picturesque buildings to finish, where the coastal path began, at the ferry terminal.

BIBLIOGRAPHY
The Isle of Wight Coastal Path, by Alan Charles, published by
  Thornhill Press
  24 Moorend Road
  Cheltenham
  Gloucestershire GL53 0EU
This includes full directions, points of historical interest, maps, sketches and suggestions for places to stay.

A set of leaflets describing the route, with maps and details of places of interest, is available from Tourist Information Centres throughout the Isle of Wight, or from
  The County Surveyor
  County Hall
  Newport
  Isle of Wight PO30 1UD

3 The Vanguard Way

The way was established and officially opened by the Vanguards Rambling Club in 1980 as part of their fifteenth anniversary celebrations. The idea of forming the club was first mooted in 1965, on a return journey from Devon made by a party of high-spirited Sunday Ramblers who were forced to share the guard's van in order to travel together. Their surroundings inspired the club's name and, as a result of the efforts of its members over the years, the Vanguard Way is now a long-distance path of over 60 miles (96 km), ideal for all walking enthusiasts keen to experience the variety of scenery embraced by the walk on its route from the suburbs to the sea.

It begins on the fringes of residential south London, outside East Croydon Station, and the first stage is an easy hike through the outskirts of Croydon until at last the suburban sprawl gives way to the more pleasing sights of the countryside. Soon it reaches the wide sweep of the North Downs, with the noisy intrusion of traffic on the M25 below you.

The village of Crockham Hill, overlooking the Weald, is an ideal spot to break your journey, with a youth hostel in its main street. Winston Churchill lived at nearby Chartwell for many years and the house became famous as his country seat. Further south, the rumble of aircraft at Gatwick Airport might disturb your calm, but not for long. Soon you are at Forest Row, a pretty Sussex village on the Eastbourne road, close to the half-way stage of the path.

The way then cuts through scenic Ashdown Forest, the largest area of uncultivated land in south-east England. Covering about 20 square miles (58 sq km) in northern east and west Sussex and once part of the much larger Wealden Forest, the area is now a mixture of high, open heathland, oak and birch woodland and clumps of pine trees dotted about this well-wooded sandstone hill region of the High Weald. Ashdown was a Royal Forest for 300 years. Now it is the well-trodden domain of the motorist and the city dweller seeking

Length 62 miles (99 km)
Start East Croydon Station
Finish Seaford Station
Going On the whole easy, with one or two short climbs
Ordnance Survey Maps 176 (start only), 187, 188, 199, 198 (finish only)
Waymarking Standard waymarking at present. It is envisaged that the Vanguards Rambling Club will, with the assistance of County Councils, provide its own waymarking throughout the route in due course

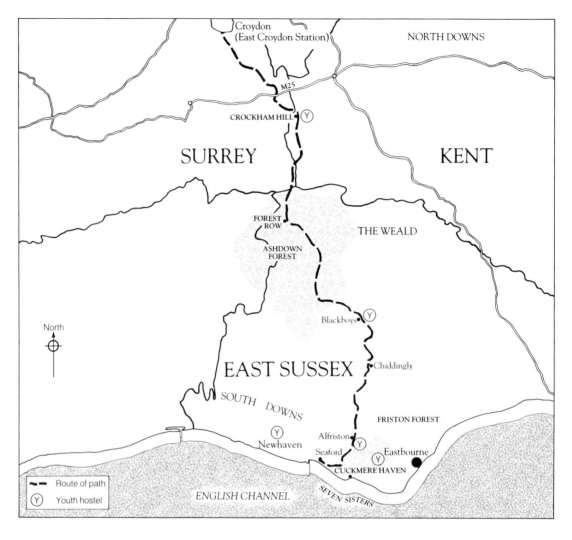

peaceful recreation in the country. Despite this invasion, it is still lovely and largely unspoilt and undiscovered in places – hard to believe that its edge is only 30 miles (48 km) from London.

Beyond the forest, the way visits Blackboys and Chiddingly, two villages with interesting tales to tell. Then it begins to head for the uncrowded expanses of the South Downs, with their summer breezes and taste of the sea. Alfriston is on the tourist trail, with its charming shops, inns and parish church, known rightly far and wide as the 'Cathedral of the Downs'. The final leg of the walk is very much Rudyard Kipling's Sussex by the sea. First, there is Friston Forest, with Westdean buried delightfully within it. Then there is Cuckmere Haven, leading to the sea at Seven Sisters, the fine, very English white chalk

Opposite Nore Hill – deep in commuter country. At last the walk turns its back on south London's sprawling environs and offers a pleasing prospect of undulating fields and woodland.

cliffs which rise out of the Channel between here and Eastbourne. The last mile or so is along the cliffs west of the Seven Sisters to Seaford Head and the small coastal town of Seaford below it.

There is a good range of accommodation on the route and plenty of inns for food and refreshment. There are also youth hostels at Crockham Hill, Blackboys and Alfriston. East Croydon is well served by buses and regular trains from Victoria. At the end of the route Seaford Station provides train services to Newhaven, Lewes (for Victoria) and Brighton. There are also regular buses, including services to Eastbourne.

East Croydon Station to Crockham Hill
15½ miles (25 km)

The bustling entrance to East Croydon Station in the heart of suburban south London is perhaps an unlikely setting to begin the Vanguard Way but the walk through the woods and well-tended avenues soon after the start is a pleasant one, to be enjoyed during any season.

The way ventures for several miles through a pleasant urban landscape of lightly wooded hills and parks and select residential housing estates amidst the trees. Lloyd Park and Coombe Woods are pleasant expanses for recreation in the middle of sprawling suburbia and Selsdon Wood Nature Reserve, with 200 acres (494 ha) of woodland acquired by the National Trust in 1935–6, provides a peaceful haven away from noise and traffic.

Leaving the nature reserve, you are at last on the edge of Greater London, Selsdon being the gateway to the green belt. The scene in front of you is now rural landscape, completely free of urban development, as the way turns its back at last on London and cuts across farmland to the hamlet of Farleigh. The name originated as Fearnlege, which is Saxon for bracken clearing. Note the eleventh-century St Mary's Church in its simple rural setting amidst farmland. It was built around 1083 and is almost completely Norman. Ravaged by fire in the mid-1960s, it was carefully restored and can be visited. The church's quiet position on the edge of the hamlet is in sharp contrast to the vast residential sprawl of the south London suburbs the way has just left behind.

From Farleigh the route is across fields and beside woodland to reach another hamlet, Chelsham, where The Bull public house can be found conveniently beside the route. Beyond Chelsham, the Vanguard Way crosses the B269 road and then enters woodland. When it emerges again, the remains of what is understood to be a wartime bomb crater can be seen in front of you as the way heads towards the top of Nore Hill, overlooking Woldingham and Warlingham – two commuter villages with confusingly similar names. The hill top here is a favourite haunt of hang-glider enthusiasts.

Soon the peace of the North Downs country is shattered as you emerge from the trees at Flint House to look down on to the busy M25, with the North Downs Way running parallel a short distance from it. These slopes over which the Vanguard Way traces its route are Oxted Downs, owned by the National Trust. Looking beyond the motorway, the residential sprawl on the far side is Oxted and Limpsfield.

The path joins the North Downs Way for a short time at the bottom of the slopes and heads east toward Titsey Park, alongside thick woodland, before the two paths split and change direction again.

Beyond where the Pilgrims' Way crosses the route is the entrance to Titsey Park and the main house, which was built in 1776 by Sir John Gresham after the original one was pulled down, can be glimpsed through the trees as the way cuts across the southern edge of the park (once the site of a Roman villa). After Titsey Park, the route unfortunately goes for a brief stretch beside the motorway and then crosses it via a bridge to run up to the tiny hamlet of Moorhouse Bank beside the A25.

North of the road again and the path crosses the London Countryway, another long-distance route of over 200 miles (320 km) devised to take walkers on a complete circuit of the metropolis. Cross the B269 at Limpsfield Chart and from here it is a short walk to Crockham Hill, where there is a pub, The Royal Oak, and a youth hostel, a fine imposing house situated in the centre of the village.

Chartwell, for over forty years the home of Sir Winston Churchill, is about a mile away and is open to visitors at certain times of the year. The rooms in the house have been allowed to remain much as they were when Churchill lived there, several becoming a museum. The studio in the garden, containing a number of Churchill's paintings, is also open to the public.

The nearby old town of Westerham boasts a bronze statue of Churchill on the green, as well as one of another notable figure, General Sir James Wolfe, who fought in the famous battle between the English and French at Quebec in 1759. Wolfe spent his formative years at Quebec House in Westerham, also owned by the National Trust.

Crockham Hill to Forest Row
12 miles (19 km)

Refreshment is limited on this stretch, with only a couple of inns to choose from at Dormansland and Marsh Green, two villages both of which are some distance from the main route of the path.

Crockham Hill provides pleasing views towards the Weald of

Kent – the next stage of the Vanguard Way. Beyond the village, the route of the walk is across flat farmland, running along the edge of the interestingly named Guildables Wood for a while before arriving a little later at Troy Town on the Tonbridge–Redhill railway line. Then, a stretch of quiet country road brings you to Haxted Mill on the River Eden. A quaint, weatherboarded building of historic interest, Haxted is a working mill incorporating a museum which is open at certain times and has a restaurant and tearoom adjoining. The

Opposite Oxted Downs above the grey thread of the M25. In the far distance, beyond the trees, lie Oxted and Limpsfield.

Haxted Mill, on the road to Edenbridge, located beside the River Eden on the site of a fourteenth-century mill.

mill was built in 1680 but has not been in commercial use since 1949.

The way continues across fields and watermeadows, probably the only sound to disturb the tranquil scene being that of air traffic circling overhead as planes take off from nearby Gatwick Airport. Very soon the elegant, graceful frontage of Starborough Castle comes into view. The house stands in spacious, well-tended grounds on the site of a Norman castle, which was garrisoned by the Parliamentarians during the Civil War and later dismantled. Only the moat remains, visible as you cross the drive leading to the house.

From here it is soon a gradual climb through woodland to meet the Sussex Border Path near the top, where there are good views towards the north and the west. For some time the Vanguard Way has been running roughly parallel with the county boundary between Surrey and Kent, crossing the line several times at Crockham Hill and Troy Town. Dropping down from the higher country to the road, a little further to the south is where the Surrey and Kent boundary meets East Sussex.

The way twists for some time through semi-wooded country and across farmland and parkland before finally reaching Forest Row. The approach into Forest Row is past the site of the old railway station on the line between Three Bridges and Tunbridge Wells. The line has now been dismantled and in its place is the Forest Way Country Park, an amenity path running for about 7 miles (11 km) between East Grinstead and Groombridge along the route of the old track.

Reaching The Foresters' Arms, you are now in the centre of Forest Row, a large, sprawling village with a number of charming houses and cottages on the A22 Eastbourne road. There are several inns and hotels in Forest Row, making it suitable for an overnight stop. The village, once an important staging post, is a popular centre for exploring Ashdown Forest. To the north are the ruins of Brambletye House, once the home of Sir James Richards, who fled the country to Spain in 1683 after being suspected of treason.

Forest Row to Blackboys
12¾ miles (20 km)

From The Foresters' Arms the path follows the B2110 road for a short distance before cutting between private gardens and along leafy roads through the quiet residential outskirts of the village.

Beyond Forest Row, the Vanguard Way emerges on to the edge of the Royal Ashdown Forest Golf course, to follow a route weaving between trees and across lush fairways. The course is prettily laid out among the trees of the forest, with good views across to the hamlets of Quabrook and Coleman's

Hatch, the tower of the modern-English-style church there rising skyward over on the far hillside. A local family of landowners who lived here were responsible for erecting a hatch or gate into the forest – hence the name Coleman's Hatch. There are many other villages and hamlets in the area that incorporate 'hatch' or 'gate' in their names, as a glance at the ordnance survey map will show.

Beyond the road leading to the Ashdown Forest Centre, which is well worth a visit, the way skirts the boundaries of a neat, well-tended bowling green, looking oddly out of place in this rather lonely forest setting. The path cuts between it and the neighbouring cricket field to reach the road at Newbridge. As you approach it, there are good views of Ashdown Forest towards Gill's Lap, the next stage of the Vanguard Way on the distant hillside.

The ford further along the road is known locally as the Splash. The stream over which the way passes begins to head

The Splash at Newbridge. The ford is near 'Pooh Sticks Bridge' of *Winnie the Pooh* fame. The hamlet of Newbridge was once the setting for the oldest iron furnace in Sussex.

Forest Row on the northern edge of the Ashdown Forest.

Opposite Forest magic. Gill's Lap, high up in the Ashdown Forest, a breezy place of wild beauty and lonely heathland. This is where the Vanguard Way was officially opened in 1980. In the distance is Five Hundred Acre Wood – the Hundred Acre Wood of the A. A. Milne stories.

across country towards Cotchford Farm, which was the home of A. A. Milne, creator of Winnie the Pooh. Devotees of Milne's enchanting stories are likely to recognize the fictional background of Pooh's haunts in the forest despite the invasion of today's tourists and traffic. For example, after the Splash the path climbs steadily through the open heathland of the forest to reach Gill's Lap, or Galleon's Lap, as it is described in Milne's *The House at Pooh Corner*.

Gill's Lap is probably one of the most famous landmarks in the forest and certainly the highest. From the top at Gill's Lap Clump, a copse once used to conceal parties of deer hunters,

Gill's Lap was the scene of a particularly intriguing murder mystery at the end of the eighteenth century. The story concerned a young apprentice and his master, a bullying tradesman, both from Tunbridge Wells. One day they came to the forest on business, travelling on foot, and afterwards journeyed home separately in order to make further calls on the way. On the return trip, a stranger asked the apprentice the time when he reached Redgate Mill near Rotherfield and was told he would soon hear the church clock strike four. The man did indeed hear the clock a few moments later. What the apprentice did not know was that his master had been savagely murdered about 4 miles (6 km) away, near Gill's Lap, while on his way home. At the time the killing appeared to be motiveless, but soon the apprentice was arrested and charged with the man's murder. Then, mysteriously, the night before the case came up, a farmer from West Hoathly was bothered in his sleep by a nagging voice urging him inexplicably to go to Lewes. Hesitant and somewhat suspicious at first, he eventually decided to go and when, on arrival, the farmer heard about the case, he immediately gave evidence to the effect that he had met the apprentice at Redgate Mill just before four o'clock on the day of the murder, making it impossible for the young man to have been responsible. Thanks to the farmer's last-minute intervention, the apprentice was acquitted.

the views are magnificent. With good visibility it is possible to see the North Downs away to the right and the South Downs on the left. On this spot in 1980, the Vanguard Way was officially opened by the National Secretary of the Ramblers' Association, making it a significant landmark on the route.

For a while now, the way follows the well-explored tourist trails of the forest and, during the summer months particularly, the route is never far from crowded picnic areas or the familiar sight of ice-cream vans.

Ashdown is one of the few remaining relics of the huge Wealden Forest which once covered a substantial part of southern England, stretching from Hampshire to East Kent. Dominated mainly by oak and beech trees, it had a long and varied history, though today there is little to see of the original forest apart from patches of woodland dotted about the Weald. Ashdown is the largest and wildest survivor. Prehistoric man hunted in this forest before the Roman invasion. The Romans successfully established a well-organized iron industry here and were also responsible for building a road through the forest. However, in the post-Roman Dark Ages, Ashdown was little disturbed by outside influences.

The route cuts through the wilderness of often barren heathland and trees and on towards King's Standing Clump, beyond where the Vanguard Way meets the Weald Way, a long-distance path of about 80 miles (128 km) across the Weald, running from Gravesend to Eastbourne. King's Standing Clump is said to be where pleasure-loving Edward II hunted deer in the fourteenth century, hiding in the small copse beyond the car park. Again, this is a favourite haunt of day-trippers and ice-cream vans in the warmer weather.

The next stretch provides spectacular views until the way leaves the forest at last and joins the A26 road at Poundgate, from where the scenery becomes softer and pastoral once more. Beyond the fields, it reaches High Hurstwood, with its ornate nineteenth-century Holy Trinity Church and 1903 tower in a quiet lane on the edge of the village. In the seventeenth century, High Hurstwood was known as Heyhurst, meaning 'high enclosed wood'. Later it became Hayhurst Wood and at one time High Heyhurstwood. The fact that 'hurst' lends itself to so many place names in this rural corner of the country is a clear indication of how extensively it was once covered by forest.

The route of the walk continues across country to pass beneath the Crowborough–Uckfield railway line. Then it is on to Pound Green, with its attractive houses and cottages spread across the hillside. The final leg to Blackboys is again across fields and through pleasantly peaceful country.

Blackboys has an interesting history and there are a number of different theories as to the origin of its name. The two explanations most popular locally suggest that it derives either from iron working and charcoal burning, both of which made workers black, or the name of a fifteenth-century squire who lived in the village, Richard Blakeboy. The local inn on the Lewes road, which was a farmhouse in the fourteenth century, shares the village's name and is reputed to be haunted by the restless spirit of the publican's daughter, who died in childbirth, having been abandoned by her lover.

Blackboys to Alfriston
14¾ miles (24 km)

The way continues to explore rural East Sussex after leaving Blackboys. It skirts Hawkhurst Common before pressing on to the tiny settlement of Graywood. Behind Graywood House, the path disappears into bluebell woods and then through private gardens to emerge at a caravan park in the fields

Opposite The Cathedral of the Downs. The spire of Alfriston's splendid parish church peeps above the trees. To the right of the church, the Cuckmere river flows serenely through its downland valley.

beyond. After a short spell beside the road, the way returns to farmland again as it heads towards the distinctive spire of Chiddingly Church, rising to 130 feet (39 m) against the splendid backdrop of the South Downs.

Chiddingly is a peaceful village, its dwellings dotted about the quiet lanes that crisscross this delightful part of the county between the Weald and the sea. The thirteenth-century church contains an imposing monument to the Jefferay family. Sadly, the memorial has been defaced, but that in itself is an interesting part of the church's history and not the work of latter-day vandals. The desecration was carried out by local people in the second half of the seventeenth century as they believed that the effigy of Sir John Jefferay related instead to the notorious 'hanging Judge Jefferies' of 'Bloody Assize' fame, even though the spelling of the name is different. The Six Bells public house is almost within the shadow of the church and conveniently placed for refreshment beside the route of the path.

Leaving Chiddingly via the churchyard, the way veers south-west over gentle farmland to join the A22 at Holme's Hill. After Limekiln Farm, the path follows a lengthy section of tree-lined path, often wet and muddy, and eventually meets the road at Chalvington. When it leaves the road again, it begins to emerge at last from the soft, wooded country of this region into more spectacular surroundings, with the broad rim of the South Downs clearly visible ahead.

The views are no less dramatic at Mays Farm, with glimpses of Arlington Reservoir on the left or as you cross the fields beyond Berwick Station, with its inn located beside the railway line. Confusingly, the station and the village of Berwick are about a mile apart, but the walk is rewarding none the less. The stretch between Berwick and Alfriston is particularly exhilarating, especially on a cool summer's day. Each season brings its own pleasures and pitfalls to walking on the Downs, but it is always a bracing experience at any time of the year, the coastal breezes often bringing with them the salty tang of the sea.

As you approach Alfriston, an unusual spectacle, almost reminiscent of a scene in Austria or Switzerland, greets you. It is a replica of the crucifix attached to a garden wall in a quiet lane overlooking the Downs. The simple inscription below it reads 'God So Loved The World' (St John, 3:16). It also proclaims that the crucifix was erected by Alice S. Gregory, 28 April 1919.

Alfriston is a mecca for tourists. They come in droves to inspect its picturesque main street and quaint old inns, including the fifteenth-century, part-timbered Star, which has a carved red lion figurehead at its corner that is believed to have come from a seventeenth-century Dutch ship wrecked

near the coast. Several inns at Alfriston once had a strong association with smuggling and the local gang made good use of the Cuckmere river, between here and the sea, by transporting their contraband upriver as far as the village.

As well as its buildings and its old market cross in Waterloo Square, Alfriston boasts another major attraction for visitors. The parish church, often described as the 'Cathedral of the Downs', dates mainly from the fourteenth century and stands on an ancient Saxon mound. Across the green from the church is the charming oak-framed, thatched Clergy House, built about 1350 to cater for a confined number of parish priests in the aftermath of the Black Death. The National Trust acquired it as their first property in 1896, paying the princely sum of £10 for the privilege.

The Star Inn at Alfriston

Alfriston to Seaford
7 miles (11 km)

Behind the church, the way crosses the Cuckmere river and follows the eastern river bank as it twists and turns southwards to the village of Litlington. The path passes through the village, with its Norman church and Plough and Harrow Inn, and then climbs the hillside above it to join forces with the South Downs Way for a mile or so. Note the familiar outline of the White Horse cut into the chalk on a distant sweep of the Downs. There are superb views from the hill back over the route of the path to Alfriston, along the banks of the Cuckmere, and in front glimpses of Friston Forest, a vast, wooded expanse of nearly 2,000 acres (4,942 ha) into which the Vanguard Way disappears.

The forest is owned by the Eastbourne Waterworks Company, though it is leased to the Forestry Commission. There are a number of waymarked trails amid the pine and beech trees and a varied range of plant and animal life. Inside the forest there are several flights of steps to negotiate before and after the pretty hamlet of Westdean, lying hidden by itself in a wooded hollow. It is a curious place to find after the bracing loftiness of the Downs – quiet and undiscovered in the trees. The church is mostly fourteenth century and the old flint rectory beside it was probably built by the Normans. Nearby, Charleston Manor has an interesting blend of Tudor and Georgian architecture and is set amid spacious gardens which are open daily in the summer. Its huge fifteenth-century tithe barn is reputed to be the largest in Sussex.

Alfred the Great is supposed to have been associated with the area. He is thought to have built a palace here, where his biographer and mentor Bishop Asser met him for the first time.

At the top of a flight of over 200 steps climbing through the trees of the forest, the path suddenly leaves Friston and emerges into open country once more. When it does so, you are looking down on Cuckmere Haven, where the river winds in erratic fashion towards the sea. Down at the road is the entrance to the Seven Sisters Country Park, an amenity area of nearly 700 acres (1,730 ha) developed by East Sussex County Council after they acquired this part of the Cuckmere Valley. The site is an ideal location for a country park and it has been thoughtfully planned to blend with the coastal beauty of this area. There are man-made lakes and a park trail starting at the main gate, and nearby an old Sussex barn has been converted to provide a park centre which includes many interesting exhibits and displays.

The way follows the road to Exceat Bridge, with the Golden Galleon Inn in solitary splendour beside it. Then it swings

The Clergy House at Alfriston. Situated on the edge of the village green, the thatched building has oak framing and wattle and daub walls. It was built in the fourteenth-century to accommodate a small knot of parish priests after the Black Death.

coastward to follow a grassy track within the boundaries of Seaford Head Nature Reserve – over 300 acres (741 ha) of remote chalk down adjoining the mouth of the Cuckmere. The path here hugs the course of the river for about a mile. Then the famous Seven Sisters Cliffs – there are, in fact, eight – slowly edge into view as the Cuckmere finally reaches the sea. At this point the path heads west along the cliff top towards Seaford Head, 282 feet (85 m) above the sea, where there is a golf course superbly situated to take advantage of the magnificent coastal scenery. Some of the best views of the Seven Sisters may be experienced from here.

Beyond the golf course, the way drops down into Seaford. As it does so, there are good views over the town towards the parish church of St Leonard's, with its sturdy fifteenth–century tower and, on the front, a surviving Martello tower, one of many built as a line of defence during the Napoleonic period. Once the port of Lewes, Seaford has always suffered with its coastal defences. Strong westerly gales tend to sweep sea water and large deposits of shingle over the sea wall towards the town.

The Vanguard Way follows the esplanade for the last stretch of its varied route, which began at East Croydon Station and finishes, appropriately, at the railway station at Seaford town centre.

BIBLIOGRAPHY
The Vanguard Way, published by the Vanguards Rambling Club, contains full directions and maps, as well as other information including a gazetteer and suggestions for places to stay, and is available from:
The Vanguards Rambling Club
109 Selsdon Park Road
South Croydon
Surrey CR2 8JJ

4 The Suffolk Coast Path

Length 50 miles (80 km)
Start Felixstowe
Finish Lowestoft
Going Easy
Ordnance Survey Maps 134, 156, 169
Waymarking Yellow arrows on a brown background

The path is over public rights of way but on certain stretches of coastline at Bawdsey and between Southwold and Kessingland access is by agreement with the landowner and therefore may be subject to diversion.

The Suffolk Coast Path begins at Felixstowe and ends at Lowestoft. Both are typical English seaside towns. They were never as fashionable as Frinton or Walton-on-the-Naze, but their popularity grew around the usual holiday attractions and they provide an ideal base for touring East Anglia. Much of this walk is over the Suffolk Heritage coast, often with only the waves of the North Sea for company as they break beside you on the shingle. For over 30 miles (48 km) the path is along a lonely, crumbling coastline that has been ravaged by the sea for centuries. Many towns and ports that were once thriving and prosperous are now little more than ruined villages and small, select holiday resorts like Aldeburgh and Walberswick cling for life in the face of relentless attack. Appropriately at Aldeburgh, a road is named after one of its most famous sons, the poet George Crabbe, who summed up the tragic plight of this area by writing: 'The ocean roar whose greedy waves devour the lessening shore'. The rivers near this coast meander for miles under huge East Anglian skies, seemingly unable to make up their minds which direction to choose. Their winding routes certainly gave eighteenth-century smugglers a great advantage over the excisemen.

Suffolk is a county strongly influenced by the sea and by the rivers and estuaries flowing into it. Before the advent of the road transport system, they were often filled with trading vessels on their way to and from the North Sea. The stretches of path by the river provide a peaceful rural alternative to the coastal sections and are equally flat underfoot, with a route taking in Tunstall Forest, the famous Snape Maltings, with its fine reputation for music, and the desolate marshes of the Walberswick Nature Reserve.

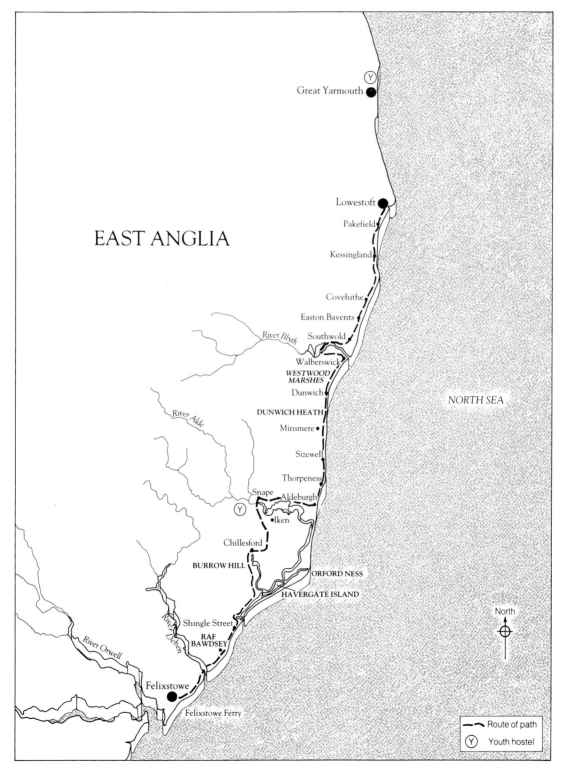

EAST ANGLIA

Great Yarmouth

Lowestoft
Pakefield
Kessingland

Covehithe

Easton Bavents

River Blyth Southwold

Walberswick
WESTWOOD MARSHES

Dunwich

DUNWICH HEATH

Minsmere

River Alde Sizewell

Thorpeness

Snape Aldeburgh

•Iken

Chillesford

BURROW HILL

ORFORD NESS

HAVERGATE ISLAND

Shingle Street
RAF BAWDSEY

River Deben

River Orwell

Felixstowe

Felixstowe Ferry

NORTH SEA

North

Route of path

Ⓨ Youth hostel

Opposite Orford Ness and Havergate Island – a low, marshy landscape of muddy lagoons, ditches and channels. Now a bird sanctuary extending over 300 acres (741 ha), the island is a desolate place, inhabited by Britain's largest breeding colony of avocets.

Whether on the coast or inland, the fine churches of Suffolk are never far away. The proud achievements of the wool merchants, they stand out for miles on the flat landscape, defying the elements, challenging the sea to destroy them.

This is not a walk just for lovers of the sea and of long, empty beaches. There are many interesting plants and birds to see on the shore and along the marshes and river estuaries. Of the wild flowers and shingle plants, purple sea lavender and the yellow horned poppy can be seen in colourful bloom, and among the birds who visit these shores are marsh harriers, avocets and terns, who breed in quiet, undisturbed surroundings.

The reedy marshes of Minsmere Nature Reserve are a haven for wildfowl, too, and keen ornithologists flock to this dry yet breezy coast. There is also much for beachcombers to find here, including amber, if only rarely, and the precious tan-coloured stone, cornelian.

Felixstowe, Aldeburgh, Southwold and Lowestoft provide a good range of hotels and guesthouses. There is also a youth hostel at Blaxhall near Snape. Trains and buses run regularly between Ipswich (on the mainline to London) and Felixstowe. There are also trains between Lowestoft and Ipswich. The ferry across to Bawdsey operates a regular service during the summer.

Felixstowe to Aldeburgh
23 miles (37 km)

Felixstowe's role as a holiday resort began during the Victorian era. These days, it is a busy ferry terminal as well, handling freight and traffic bound for the Continent. It is hard to believe that there was once a Roman fort here, now lying submerged beneath the waters of the North Sea.

From the car park in Cliff Road, overlooking the sea, the path follows the sea wall north towards Felixstowe Ferry. Almost at once two common landmarks along this coast come clearly into view: the Martello Towers. They were built in the nineteenth century as a precaution against Napoleonic attack and over 100 of them were strategically placed along the east and south coasts, between Aldeburgh in Suffolk and Seaford in Sussex. Their origin can be traced to Martella in Corsica, where battle defences of this kind came under heavy cannon fire from the British in 1794. Today they still watch over the sea, but more as silent monuments of the past.

At Felixstowe Ferry, pass alongside the Sailing Club and Boatyard and take the quaint little ferry boat across the estuary of the River Deben to Bawdsey on the opposite bank (it is advisable to check the times of sailings by telephone beforehand). The entrance to RAF Bawdsey is immediately in front of you as you step ashore. This side of the river and the

coastline beyond is owned by the Ministry of Defence and it was here that early research into radar was carried out. The bustle of Felixstowe Ferry and the glimpses of life at Bawdsey Manor seem to be in sharp contrast to what lies ahead, for the next stretch of the coast path is along lonely, deserted beaches with precious few reminders of any civilization. Much of the coastline here is neglected and forgotten by time. With the beaches often quite overgrown in places, one could be forgiven for thinking that not a living soul had passed this way for years.

Occasionally, the route stumbles upon a lonely outpost along the shoreline. Shingle Street, appropriately named, is an isolated row of houses and bungalows, seemingly cut off from the rest of the world and, with people's homes facing directly on to the beach, left to battle with the elements as best it can. There are no proper facilities here and it is not a place for the faint-hearted; ony brave souls with a love of the sea stay here.

At Shingle Street the path cuts inland for about a mile by way of a single-track road. Then a distinctive ladder stile comes into view up ahead beside a bridge. Cross the stile and follow the river path, briefly heading back towards the coast. It soon veers north again in the direction of Orford.

The path meanders for miles beside winding water margins and creeks. The view is predominantly a mixture of sea and desolate marshy landscape, with Orford Ness and Havergate Island in the near distance. Orford Ness is a long, natural barrier of shingle swept up by the sea, now forming one of the largest spits in the country, though in medieval times it reached no further south than Orford itself. Nowadays, it is about 5 miles (8 km) longer than it was then. The sea might have hungrily claimed much of the coastline in this quiet corner of the country over the years, but here at Orford it has generously given something back.

Alongside Orford Ness, just across the water, can be seen the low shape of Havergate Island, which is really nothing more than a shingle ridge, so bleak and barren that it could almost be the surface of another planet. The only signs of life come from its regular visitors, breeding birds including the avocet, a wading bird with an upward, curving bill that has nested here since the late 1940s. The island may be a remote, undisturbed nature reserve now but once it was a refuge for smugglers and it is easy to understand why, for not only was Havergate superbly isolated but when the smugglers had got this far, the perils of the sea at least were behind them.

Some time later the path turns away from the coast again and climbs Burrow Hill. From the top there are good views back across the Ness, the estuary, over Havergate Island and the route of the path generally, stretching back towards Felixstowe. There are signs on Burrow Hill of recent archaeological excavations, which confirmed that there was once a Saxon settlement here. From the top the way follows a route through typical English agricultural and woodland scenery before reaching the village of Chillesford.

Then the path is through Tunstall Forest, lined with uniform rows of Corsican pines, and the ground is often carpeted with cones. Beyond the forest, the walk emerges into more open country, bringing you eventually to the banks of the River Alde at a particularly scenic stretch known as Cliff Reach. The river is so wide at this point that you coud be forgiven for thinking it was a lake. Much of the south bank is an area of heaths, commonland and scattered clusters of houses and cottages buried down quiet lanes. Collectively, it is known as

At Snape Maltings these days there are farm and craft shops, galleries and wine bars, and you can take river trips from here. There is also a piano workshop and the Britten–Pears Music School for Advanced Musical Studies, dedicated to the memory of the festival founders, Benjamin Britten and Peter Pears. The nineteenth-century buildings on the banks of the Alde once bustled with activity of a different kind, as malt was produced from Suffolk barley and then shipped out to the North Sea, thanks to Newson Garrett, who created a malting business here in 1841. His daughter, Elizabeth Garrett Anderson, became the first woman in Britain to qualify as a doctor and a hospital in London is named after her.

Sadly, the discovery of the value of road transport put paid to the future of the Maltings and they eventually fell into decline. But in those early days when workers busily toiled in the old buildings, now clad with creeper, little did they imagine that over 100 years later Snape Maltings would become an international music venue, with opera and jazz, as well as a centre for antique fairs and TV events. A converted windmill at Snape was the home of Benjamin Britten during the 1930s and 1940s and he wrote *Peter Grimes* here. There is also an old smugglers' inn nearby which had peepholes so that a watch could be maintained across the river marshes and a windowless room upstairs, used by smugglers as a refuge where they could stay undetected. Over 250 years ago, when smuggling was common in this area, bribes were paid to preventive men to look the other way. Those who did not were likely to come to a bad end, or to be chased, as one man was, to Snape in order to have his nose cut off.

Snape Maltings – home of the Aldeburgh Festival. Set prettily amid the salt marshes of the Alde, the Maltings are synonymous with music. The concert hall was converted in 1967 and restored in 1970 following a fire.

Opposite The lesser-known face of the Maltings – a delightful collection of granaries and Victorian ivy-clad buildings in which malt was once produced from Suffolk barley.

Iken, though individually there is Iken Heath, Iken Common, Iken Boot and, where the path meets the river, Iken Cliff.

Looking along Cliff Reach beyond the anchored boats and mudflats, a church tower peeps into view near the end of the opposite headland. This is St Botolph's, which once boasted a thatched roof, until it was destroyed by fire in 1968. The church dates from 1300 and at one time stood on an island which could be reached only on foot at low tide. In the eighteenth and nineteenth centuries, Iken was quite an important fishing village and the Alde was often busy with shipping. An Orford-family-run business traded from Iken Cliff between 1780 and 1860, mainly in coal, corn, lime and general cargo, and Ketch barges used the river as far as Snape, a mile away, until early this century. Watch closely for signs of wildlife along this stretch of the Alde, including herons, redshanks and shelducks.

With frequent glimpses of Snape Maltings beyond the salt marshes, the route keeps to the same path until it joins the road at Snape village. Turn right and on your right almost immediately is the rambling, world-famous Snape Maltings complex. It is worth a pause and perhaps a drink at the aptly named Plough and Sail pub right beside it, for there is much

more to see than just the renowned Concert Hall, centre of the Aldeburgh Festival since 1967.

Leaving Snape, the path returns towards the Alde, this time following the north bank, known locally as Sailors' Path. When it joins the road, you are on the outer reaches of Aldeburgh. This is an attractive old town, much of which has been washed away by the sea over the years, but it still boasts some fine houses and historic buildings. The sixteenth-century Moot Hall, which is timber-framed, is now practically on the beach. It used to be in the middle of the town, but the constantly shifting shoreline has resulted in this change of position. Aldeburgh used to be an important coastal fishing village, specializing in herring, but these days it is little more than a quiet seaside resort, renowned for the annual music festival held every June which was begun by Benjamin Britten in 1948. To visit the town, follow the road towards the sea-front from the direction of the Sailors' Path. Continuing the Suffolk Coast Path, take Golf Lane on the other side of the main road leading to Aldeburgh.

Aldeburgh to Southwold
15 miles (24 km)

Half-way down the lane, next to the golf course, is The Red House, home of Benjamin Britten until his death in 1976. He lived here with his great friend and companion, Peter Pears, who died ten years later. Opposite the entrance to the house, the route of the way leaves the lane and crosses the fairway as waymarked. Follow the path across the marshes to rejoin the beach north of Aldeburgh. A pleasant walk along the coast here brings into view the houses and bungalows of Thorpeness.

It is worth deviating from the route for a brief look at the village, which was specifically designed as a seaside resort during the Edwardian era and has much of architectural interest to see – in particular, the famous 'House in the Clouds', which has been photographed a good deal over the years and is, in fact, an old water tower cunningly disguised as a house. There is a nineteenth-century working windmill, too, which is also the venue for the local Heritage Coast Centre, another one of which can be found further along the route at Walberswick.

Returning to the beach and a little further on, the grim, grey outline of Sizewell A nuclear power station gradually appears. Even on a sunny day, it looks cheerless, ugly and inhospitable, occupying an incongruous position right alongside the foreshore. Built in 1958, Sizewell A uses 27 million tons of seawater per hour to cool the reactors. The water is then fed back into the sea via two structures resembling offshore oilrigs. The new Sizewell B complex is due to be completed by the mid-1990s.

There is a small village lying in the shadow of Sizewell

which, together with the beach and the treacherous seas along this part of the coastline, has long been associated with smuggling.

Also to be found within sight of the power station is Minsmere Bird Reserve, just behind the beach. This is a paradise not only for rare birds but also for ornithologists, many of whom can often be seen standing motionless with their sophisticated binoculars to hand, gazing out across the marshes or emerging from the well-positioned hides situated along the path. A more revealing view of Minsmere may be had from the top of the cliffs, further along the shore.

It is a short climb to Dunwich Heath on the cliff top, where there is the inevitable car park, but the heath itself is such a stunning carpet of bright-purple heather that it tends to overshadow everything else. Dunwich Heath, owned by the National Trust, covers 214 acres (529 ha) of sandy cliffs and heathland, a mile of shingle beach and the foreshore below high-water mark.

From here it is a relatively short walk down into Dunwich village. This was once a medieval port of some size and

Sizewell beach – longshore fishing craft pulled up in the sinister shadow of Sizewell A nuclear power station. The huge complex dominates this stretch of the coast. Smuggling was once a regular activity here and during one night an astonishing 8,000 gallons of gin were brought ashore.

The relic of an old drainage mill on Westwood Marshes. At one time this entire fen landscape was littered with such mills, erected to drain the marshes. This one had sails until they were destroyed by fire some years ago.

importance, with as many as nine churches, but a terrible storm in 1326 caused considerable damage and flooding, destroying much of the community, and after that the town was never quite the same again. Further storms and continual erosion of the coast here over the years, particularly between the sixteenth and eighteenth centuries, when as much as 1,000 feet (303 m) of land was lost to the sea, has weakened the resolve of people to stay. Now, present-day Dunwich is little more than a lonely seaside village beside a shingle beach. It is a haunting sort of place and by visiting the little museum which tells the tragic fate of the community, it is possible to evoke images of a once-bustling, prosperous town, much of which stood where the waves now break against the shoreline. It has been said by local people that the bells of the lost churches can still be heard ringing beneath the waves. It would be nice to believe the claim, but even if it is not true, it still makes for a wonderful story, full of ghostly atmosphere and imagination.

In the village pub, The Ship Inn, which is the last watering hole before the walk to Walberswick, a poster on the wall draws your attention to a reward of £500 for any information leading to the seizure of a ship that had been used for smuggling in the area. The poster is dated October 1782.

Leaving the village street of quaint old houses, the route is now along the edge of Dunwich Forest, for some a pleasing alternative to the long trek over the shingle banks from Aldeburgh, however enjoyable and exhilarating. The path soon changes direction to head back towards the coastline, leaving the trees to skirt round the edge of Westwood Marshes. As at Orford Ness, it is a flat, empty landscape of winding rivers and dykes, and for me it conjures up the same images of smuggling and ancient tales of mystery on this lonely stretch of coast. Beyond the marshes, which are part of the Walberswick National Nature Reserve and protected by the Nature Conservancy Council, the way reaches Walberswick village, a pretty little place with a green and a number of houses of great charm and character. As with so many towns that once prospered on the East Anglian coast, the sea at Walberswick has brought an irreversible decline in fortune and now it is just a quiet, peaceful village lying in the shadow of Southwold, a mile away across the estuary of the Blyth.

The harbour at Southwold is simple and quite quaint. The ferry service across the river is available only at certain times and it may be necessary to walk upstream and cross the river by the footbridge. Returning on the opposite bank, the route heads north again into Southwold, towards the 100-ft (30-m) white-walled lighthouse standing sentinel above the town. It is a very useful landmark, not only for shipping, and can be seen by day and night from virtually all parts of Southwold.

The route of the way passes Gun Hill, overlooking the sea where six cannon stand silently defending the town. It is thought they were presented to Southwold by the Duke of Cumberland, who landed here from Flanders in the eighteenth century on his way to Scotland to fight Bonnie Prince Charlie. Once a Saxon fishing port, the town is particularly attractive, with a network of picturesque streets and as many as nine greens, which mark the areas where a terrible fire swept through Southwold in 1659, destroying over 200 homes. The seafront, with its huts, Victorian terraces and sand and shingle

Shining Beacon. Southwold lighthouse dominates the town.

– 89 –

beach, still seems to convey a genteel, dignified air of Edwardian gaiety.

Southwold to Lowestoft
12 miles (19 km)

After Southwold the path continues along the beach. Note the signs beside the sea wall, which indicate the route of the way from this point as far as Kessingland. It is advisable to check the tides before setting out on this leg of the walk. If necessary, take the alternative inland route via Reydon, Easton Bavents, then to the west of Easton Broad and on to Covehithe and Benacre Broad.

This stretch of coastline as far as Kessingland is one of the most spectacular parts of the whole walk, with low, sandy cliffs, striking woodland scenery, several shallow Suffolk broads and the occasional dwelling or church tower peeping through the trees, as at Covehithe, a tiny village several miles beyond Southwold.

The town and the lighthouse linger behind you on the Southwold Common. On the left are the town's two distinctive, almost futuristic, water towers and just to the right of them is the 100-foot (30-m) tower of the parish church of St Edmund – one of Southwold's finest treasures and a reminder of the former prosperity of the region.

Opposite River Blyth and the Saxon fishing port of Southwold. An artist attempts to capture the romantic flavour of this bustling river scene. The little rowing boat crossing the Blyth is the ferry between Walberswick and Southwold harbour.

River Blyth lined with boatyards and little huts selling fresh fish. The river foreshore is muddy, with particularly strong currents. On the opposite bank is Southwold harbour.

Opposite Benacre Beach. This is a particularly lonely stretch of coastline, thankfully inaccessible by car. Benacre Ness is one of the most easterly points in England, second only to Lowestoft Ness, a few miles to the north.

horizon long after you have left Southwold but soon there are other diversions. In a gap in the cliffs is Benacre Broad. Almost completely surrounded by trees and a haven for wildfowl, it seems a tranquil alternative to the dramatic spectacle of the sea, sometimes wild and magnificent, sometimes moody and sullen, but never dull. Along this part of the Suffolk coast during the summer months, terns may be found nesting. They breed in colonies around the shores of Britain and signs urge you to take care, as these birds are vulnerable to human disturbance and coastal development.

Kessingland is a small-town holiday base with a caravan site beyond the dunes. Past the village, which used to be the summer home of the writer Rider Haggard, the way climbs to the top of Kessingland and Pakefield Cliffs for the final, if somewhat less interesting, stretch of the walk. It may be easier to follow the foreshore at this point as the cliff-top path can sometimes be rather overgrown in places.

The promenade and seafront buildings at Lowestoft are visible now as the Suffolk Coast Path goes beside the beach towards the Claremont Pier and Kensington Gardens. It

finishes just beyond the gardens at South Pier, beside the harbour and the swing bridge. South of the harbour it is all seafront hotels and gardens, bathing chalets and amusement arcades. Beyond the bridge is the nerve centre of a busy and important fishing port, with its bustling harbour on the estuary of the River Lothing. The railway station at Lowestoft is a short distance from the end of the walk.

BIBLIOGRAPHY
A leaflet including a general description of the walk plus a map and sketches is available from:
    Suffolk County Council Planning Dept
    St Edmund House
    Rope Walk
    Ipswich
    Suffolk IP4 1LZ

5 The Yoredale Way

The Yoredale Way was pioneered in the late 1970s by writer and walking enthusiast Ken Piggin and members of the Ebor Acorn Rambling Club. 'Yore' is the earliest recorded name of the river which, since the fifteenth century, has been known as the Ure.

For nearly 100 miles (160 km) the Yoredale Way acts as a loyal companion to the Ure as it heads upstream from the Ouse, through the Yorkshire Dales, to its source on the northern boundary of the 680-square-mile (1,761-sq-km) national park. Fortunately for the walker, the route of the path and the meandering river capture the essence of Yorkshire – a land of snug cottages, drystone walls and numerous tumbling waterfalls.

The Yoredale Way is deceptive. Near the start the going is easy, gentle, undemanding and even uninspiring in places. By the finish, however, you are in a fierce, relentless world of rugged mountain landscapes and high, sweeping fells – Pennine country. The route begins in York and quickly makes for tame river scenery ambling lazily along the banks of the Ouse and the Ure, often with only anglers and kingfishers for company. The way keeps pace with the Ure through Boroughbridge, past Newby Hall and on to Ripon, the smallest cathedral city in Yorkshire. Still the landscape is pleasingly flat and pastoral. But the scene gradually changes. Beyond the village of Masham, with its enormous market square reminiscent of those found in Normandy, the way heads for the crisp, clean air of the Dales, with their magnificent broad valleys, fundamentally unchanged by the years.

Leyburn is undistinguished as a town but its setting, overlooking Wensleydale, is superb. The path outside the town known as the Leyburn Shawl provides some of the best views. West of Leyburn the horizon is soon dominated by the outline of Pen Hill. At over 1,700 feet (515 m) high, it sits majestically above the charming villages of West Witton, West Burton and Wensley. Aysgarth Falls, a captivating feature of Yorkshire, are

Length 100 miles (160 km)
Start York
Finish Kirkby Stephen
Going Initially flat, easy walking but much tougher in its latter stages
Ordnance Survey Maps 91, 98, 99, 105
Outdoor Leisure Map 30 – Yorkshire Dales (North & Central)
Waymarking Standard waymarking and infrequent yellow arrows, some with 'Yoredale Way' lettering incorporated within them

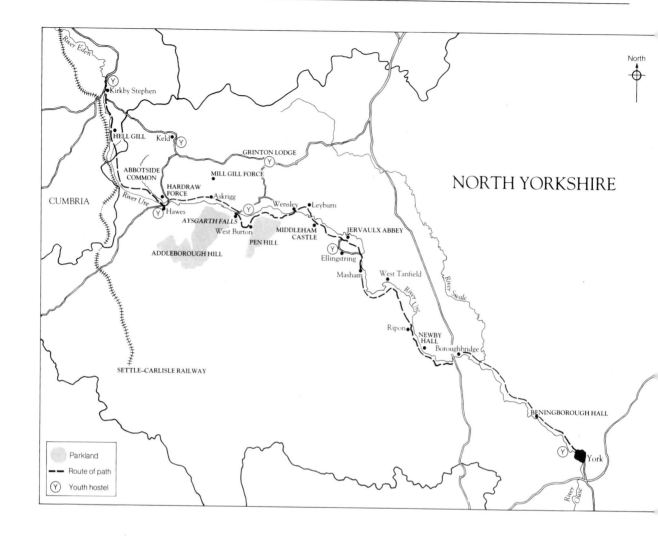

NORTH YORKSHIRE

proudly promoted by the tourist boards. Heavily commercialized, they inevitably draw large numbers of visitors. The nearby town of Askrigg is quieter but surely recognizable to eagle-eyed television viewers as fictional Darrowby in *All Creatures Great and Small*. Beyond it, hidden by trees, is Mill Gill Force, a waterfall with a wonderfully Victorian atmosphere not easily put into words. It is an enchanting place. Miss it at your peril.

From Mill Gill Force the walk to Hawes is open and sometimes bleak but the going is quite flat. The towering saddles of the Pennines are now distantly visible and soon the way reaches Hawes, at the foot of the hills. The town is convenient for an overnight stop, having a good range of accommodation. Here you can pause to lick your wounds

before tackling the last leg of the walk, physically the most gruelling of all.

High up in this remote landscape, 2,000 feet (606 m) above sea level on Abbotside Common, is the source of the River Ure. It is unusually close to the source of another river, the Eden, which flows in the opposite direction, heading north-west to feed eventually into the Solway Firth. Down below, the valley of the Eden offers a greater degree of shelter and protection

York Minster – focal point of this ancient city of riches. The minster is the mother church of the northern province of the Church of England. The majestic west towers are about 184 feet (58 m) high.

before bringing this spectacular walk to an eagerly anticipated finish at Kirkby Stephen, a pleasant little market town a few miles over the Yorkshire boundary into Cumbria.

Accommodation, including youth hostels, is quite plentiful in the main towns and villages along the route. York is easy to get to by train, bus or coach. A limited bus service operates in Kirkby Stephen at the end of the walk. The town is also on the Settle–Carlisle railway line.

York to Boroughbridge
20 miles (32 km)

York can absorb your interest for days, distracting you even before the walk has begun. There are many who regard this

The Shambles – one of the best-preserved medieval streets in Europe. This was once the street of butchers, with meat displayed on hooks outside. The overhanging buildings created dense shadows, enabling the meat to remain in the cooling shade for much of the day.

ancient Roman city as the jewel in Yorkshire's crown and they are not far wrong. Its historic attractions are too numerous to chronicle here, but among the most notable must surely be the city walls, upon which visitors can still walk and glimpse some of the best views of York, and the maze of quaint medieval streets and alleyways, in particular the Shambles, where the buildings are so close that from some of the upstairs windows you may lean out and almost touch the hand of your opposite neighbour. The most glittering of all York's treasures is, of course, its minster. Built between 1220 and 1470, it is the largest medieval church in all of northern Europe. Architecturally, it is a priceless, breathtaking work of art, visible from almost every part of the city and dominating all other buildings in sight. A major fire caused serious damage in 1984 but thankfully failed to destroy it.

This beautiful city has a history stretching back 2,000 years, but it is not just a place of celebrated monuments to the past. York is stylish, sophisticated and vibrant, with a positively cosmopolitan air about it. Thousands of people from all parts of the world stroll along its streets of fine churches and elegant buildings. They come, too, to visit the National Railway Museum, the Viking Centre and much more besides. But enough of York and on with the walk.

From the minster, walk down to Lendal Bridge, where there are boats for hire and plenty of pleasure craft negotiating this stretch of the River Ouse. The way crosses Lendal Bridge and then follows the river bank towards the railway bridge, with York City Rowing Club on the left-hand side. Follow the line of the railway embankment and continue on to a grassy path beside the river. Along this stretch there are regular glimpses of trains coming in and out of York Station and back over to your right, you have good views of the minster towering over the city. The path continues to the next road bridge, Clifton Bridge. Turn right here and cross over the river, heading towards the entrance to York Youth Hostel, a short distance further up among the trees.

Drop down under the bridge and then turn right and continue beside the river, this time on the right-hand bank. Soon the Ouse begins to sweep away to the left, with the path running beside it. Here the river acts as a boundary between urban and rural landscapes. On the far bank there are views of suburban semis with a smattering of industrial sites further on, while on this side of the river the scene is tranquil farmland, trees and hedgerows as far as the eye can see. This section also provides final glimpses of York Minster over on the backward horizon.

The path continues along the river bank, under a bridge carrying the busy A1237 road. When the traffic noise has faded for good, the placid sounds of the countryside are restored once more – the gently lapping waters of the Ouse over to the left and the swaying branches of the bushes and the trees overhanging the river. It is indeed a delightful scene.

Further on, the way enters a wooded stretch beside the Ouse, passing a detached bungalow with direct views over the river. Launches and luxurious motor cruisers are often seen gliding along this pretty reach, with cattle looking on over on the far bank. The way passes under the east coast mainline railway to Scotland and skirts open farmland along either clear paths or field boundaries but always keeping the river on the left. Occasionally anglers will suddenly peep into view along the river banks. You can stumble upon them almost without realizing – silent, motionless figures seated among the reeds and foliage.

Beningborough is hardly a village, and is really just a tiny smattering of cottages and houses overlooking the river. Beyond it the scene is typically rural – flat, agricultural land bordering the Ouse. The path now skirts the grounds of Beningborough Hall, with glimpses of the house in its very English parkland setting between rows of sturdy beech and sycamore trees. In the care of the National Trust since the late 1950s, Beningborough is a fine Georgian house designed by an unknown architect and once owned by the Earl and Countess of Chesterfield. It eventually passed to the National Trust in lieu of death duties. The house, set in over 300 acres (741 ha), contains exquisite woodcarving and a fine collection of paintings on loan from the National Portrait Gallery. Many other treasures are also on show. Beningborough Hall and its grounds are open to the public for much of the year. Access is further on along the walk.

The path swings to the right now and the Ouse is joined at this point by the River Nidd. There are still views of Beningborough Hall through the trees on the right. On the horizon the tall, ornate spire of All Saints Church, Newton, peeps into view, with its 150-feet high (45-m) Norman tower looking out over vast Yorkshire landscapes. Newton-upon-Ouse is a pretty village, with the entrance to Beningborough Hall at one end and the well-placed Dawnay Arms at the other. The inn is just down from the church, at the northern end of the village.

From here the way is now across country, through fields and rough pasture near the winding River Kyle, a little-known tributary of the Ouse. At length the path crosses the river by means of an ancient humpbacked bridge that looks as old as the landscape around it. Once across it, proceed up the track and then bear left before the farm buildings into the lane. The slender spire of Newton church is still visible along this stretch.

Turn right on joining the lane and follow it to Youlton, about 2 miles (3 km) away, passing several farms en route.

Beyond the farms it is a muddy track as far as Youlton, a tiny village of pretty stone houses and cottages on a corner of the road. Follow the road briefly and then take a track on the right. A clear sign with the heading 'Yoredale Way' announces that this is not a public path but the public may use it by permission of the owner of the land, Grimsthorpe and Drummond Castle Trust Ltd. Keep to this well-defined track for some time until it joins the road and then turn left for Aldwark, a quiet village on a bank of the Ouse.

Turn right in the village centre by The Bay Horse Inn and follow the bridle road across country, between trees and hedgerows. Over on the horizon to the right is the distant ridge of the North Yorkshire Moors, tantalizingly close for those of us who love them so much. When the track eventually reaches the road by some old beech trees, look again to the Moors for the faint outline of a horse carved into Roulston Scar. This is the nineteenth-century White Horse of Kilburn. The village below it was where Robert Thompson, a renowned woodcarver was born in 1876. His signature was also in the form of a mouse – the expression 'as poor as a Church mouse' apparently giving him the inspiration.

Turn left and head down to Myton-on-Swale, a pretty village with a straight street of old houses and cottages, the remains of an old pump house and a small church. The track at

The market cross at Boroughbridge.

the end of the main street almost immediately takes the Yoredale Way over the Swale. The wide bridge looks somewhat dilapidated these days but the river is impressive as it winds lazily through the countryside, seen here in all its varied beauty.

The route follows a raised, waymarked path across fields and meadows beside the Swale to reach the Ure. The path turns west here and follows the river bank towards Boroughbridge, passing Ellenthorpe Hall. Away in the distance across the fields on the opposite bank is the village of Aldborough, nestling among the trees. The village was once the setting for a great Roman settlement, Isurium Brigantum.

Follow the waymarkers to Milby Lock and then continue along the riverside path into Boroughbridge town centre. Boroughbridge is quiet, almost forgotten, now that the town thankfully has a by-pass to carry the thundering traffic of the A1 away from its winding streets and quaint old buildings, but at one time it had over twenty inns. The bridge over the Ure helped to establish the town in Norman times and the overly ornate market cross in the square is worth a look. The inscription reads: 'Erected 1875 by many friends in memory of the kindly virtues of Andrew Shurlock Lawson of Aldborough Manor, Esq. JP. Born 1824. Died 1872'. With several hotels, guesthouses and inns, Boroughbridge is an obvious choice for the first overnight stop on the walk.

Boroughbridge to Masham
20 miles (32 km)

Follow a wide track westwards out of Boroughbridge as far as the outer fringes of the town. Here, across the fields, the Devil's Arrows stand sentinel against the intrusive backdrop of the A1, combining a curious mix of ancient and modern. The huge prehistoric monoliths, between 18 and 22 feet (5.5 and 7 m) high, are thought to be 3,000 years old, but their origins are a mystery. Ancient mythology suggests that they were bolts used by the Devil to shoot at neighbouring cities and communities.

Turn right at the road junction and pass beneath the A1, with its deafening roar of traffic. Very quickly the way returns to the peace of the countryside again, following tracks and muddy paths between fields as far as the village of Roecliffe. The way can be quite overgrown in places along this stretch.

Walk up to the village green, which is surrounded by many charming houses and cottages. Outside the parish church of St Mary is a welcome seat with an inscription denoting Roecliffe's distinction as the Best-Kept Village in the Lower Dales in 1971. The only sound to disturb the silence here, apart from usual village activity, might be the swift, sudden roar of low-flying

The curious Devil's Arrows to the west of Boroughbridge. These prehistoric monuments, weighing 36 tons each, are probably 3,000 years old. Legend claims they were bolts shot by the Devil to destroy ancient cities.

jets, a frequent intrusion in this part of Yorkshire, or perhaps the more acceptable bleating of sheep grazing in the fields beside the church. There is an inn at Roecliffe further along the street.

Resuming the walk, follow a path beside the church and down through the fields to the river bank. For the next few miles, as far as Ripon in fact, the way keeps close to water – to begin with beside the Ure and then along the banks of the Ripon Canal. The path crosses endless fields and meadows interspersed with stretches of woodland. Pass the locks at Newby over a series of stiles and on towards the city. Soon the grounds of Newby Hall come into view over on the right bank. Strolling visitors and a miniature railway can be glimpsed across the water and then Newby Hall itself comes into view beyond the beautifully landscaped terraced gardens. The setting overlooking the Ure is glorious and the view from the river bank, so perfectly balanced and symmetrical, could be straight from a book on historic houses and gardens. Generally considered to be among Robert Adam's finest works, Newby Hall contains a feast of sumptuous tapestries, paintings and Chippendale furniture. The house is privately owned but is open to the public between April and October.

The way parts company with the river bank briefly, only to return to it at a wide, scenic reach of the gently winding Ure, from where there are good views back to Newby Hall. At Ox Close Locks the way leaves the river again and follows the Ripon Canal, crossing it by an old bridge further along. The route now follows the towpath on the eastern bank, skirting the tip of Ripon Racecourse just through the hedge on the right.

Beyond the private moorings of Ripon Motorboat Club the way reaches Rhode's Field Lock and then joins the B6265 road on the outskirts of Ripon. Turn left and follow the road towards the city centre. Ultimately the route arrives at the

It is peaceful here now but this stretch of the river near Newby Hall witnessed a terrible tragedy in the winter of 1869. A fox being chased by the hunt crossed the river at this point with Sir Charles Slingsby and other huntsmen in hot pursuit in a ferry boat. As they made their way to the opposite bank, one of the horses tried to jump out of the boat and immediately became trapped by the ropes and chains. Quickly the boat capsized and Sir Charles and five other passengers were drowned. A memorial in the grounds of Newby Hall commemorates the disaster.

cathedral church of St Peter and St Wilfred, otherwise known as Ripon Minster. Inspecting the minster from the Borough-bridge road does not do it justice. You are suddenly upon it, the huge building hemmed in by tight, narrow streets and alleyways as you gaze up from the pavement at the vertical west front and its beautifully Early English craftsmanship. Originally an Anglo-Saxon church stood on the site of the present cathedral. Only the crypt still survives.

Opposite the cathedral is the Old Courthouse, *circa* 1830, the site of the Palace of the Archbishops of York. A few minutes' walk from this spot is Ripon's rectangular market square, with its 90-feet-high (27-m) obelisk and medieval Wakeman's House, where the wakeman or night watchman lived. His task was to guard the townsfolk from robbers – an ancient form of today's Neighbourhood Watch scheme. The charming 1,000-year-old

Opposite Newby Hall. With its perfectly manicured lawns and extensive herbaceous borders sloping down to the Ure, this is a horticulturalist's paradise. The fine Adam house contains many treasures, notably the Tapestry Room and the Roman Sculpture Galleries.

West Tanfield. The picturesque village clings to the bank of the Ure. With its pretty bridge, cluster of stone cottages and tranquil setting beside the river, this is an ideal place in which to break your journey.

tradition of a horn-blower sounding a forest horn nightly at nine o'clock is still upheld. Watch out for daily tours of the city and its many attractions.

Continuing the Yoredale Way, the path strides out of the city in a northerly direction beside the Ure once again. Before long the way heads through an area of delightful parkland including several lakes and one or two bursts of woodland on the west bank of the river. Two farms, South and North Parks, lie more or less at each end of Ripon Parks and are encountered by the Yoredale Way on its journey towards Masham.

The path meets the main road at North Stainley, where there are several inns. Beyond the village the way passes Sleningford Grange and then goes on to Sleningford Mill. The approach to West Tanfield is in the form of an idyllic riverside walk with the quaint old stone bridge up ahead carrying the A6108 road into this charming village.

The street leading to the church has a row of picturesque cottages and beyond the church itself is the fifteenth-century Marmion Tower. This splendid old gatehouse with its oriel window is all that remains of the Marmion family seat. The Marmions first came here in 1215 and there are monuments to them in the church, where they are buried. Now in the care of English Heritage, the Marmion Tower is open to the public and you may climb the spiral staircase to the top for superb views over the village and the nearby river – the scene witnessed from here particularly memorable on a sunny day. However, it would be advisable to leave your possessions below, as climbing the narrow, restricted staircase in cumbersome walking boots and with an awkward rucksack heavy on your back is not the easiest task to undertake. On the corner of the street is The Bull should you be in need of sustenance before resuming your journey.

Return to the bridge and then take the track across country towards a farm, bearing left just before it to go through the fields beside the river. The path now climbs up through the trees, clinging to the banks of the Ure. Glancing back at this point, there are good views over towards West Tanfield and, nearer at hand, new vistas reveal a spectacular, gloriously wooded reach of the river.

Arriving in Mickley, you cannot fail to be impressed by its long main street of houses and bungalows and the little village church with its slate roof nestling among them. The way passes the dog kennels at the far end of the village and then goes up the hill to join a footpath leading into Hackfall Woods. The path runs parallel with the Ure and though the frolicsome river is far below you, the sound of it is quite plain at times as it races through the wooded gorge. In any season this is a delightful stretch of the walk, but it is often extremely wet and muddy in places. The way ahead is somewhat vague and

unclear but keep to the main route if you can, avoiding all the numerous branch paths.

Eventually the path breaks from the trees and continues with the Ure nearly as far as Masham, with the tall fifteenth-century spire of St Mary's Church visible for some miles.

The walk enters Masham by way of the churchyard, emerging beyond it into the huge market square. Overlooked by The Kings Head Hotel, the square is the main focal point of the village, though there is no longer a market here, simply a cross and maypole. There are shops, hotels and guesthouses, but above all Masham is famous to beer-drinkers as the home of the Theakstons' brewery.

Marmion Tower. The medieval gateway-tower is the last surviving relic from the old home of the Marmion family. Climbing the spiral staircase to the top of the tower is a worthwhile experience. From here there are delightful views of West Tanfield and beyond.

Masham to West Witton
20 miles (32 km)

From Masham head along the A6108 for a short stretch and then at the road bridge bear left. Follow the river through fields and meadows. This section of the route is well waymarked. The path meanders beside the Ure for a while, eventually coming to several farms, Low and High Mains. About a mile beyond the second farm is Low Ellington, but don't be fooled. It is not a village, just a couple of cottages and some farm buildings.

A track leads walkers to the riverbank once more and from here the route runs adjacent to the Ure for some time. When it becomes a wide, clear track, follow it to the road at Kilgram Grange. After about ½ mile (0.8 km) the way enters the grounds of Jervaulx Park, following the private drive as it cuts between mooching sheep and cattle and acres of pastureland and trees before reaching the ruins of Jervaulx Abbey over on the right. This is all that remains of an old Cistercian monastery founded in 1156. In spite of the ruins and the trees and weeds growing freely among them, the ground plan can still be identified.

Follow the drive to the road and then turn right and walk along the verge for about 1,200 feet (364 m) before taking a track leading to the river. Keep to the river bank as the way runs along a broad, clear grassy path. The sturdy nineteenth-century church tower at East Witton peeps into view on the left.

The road bridge a little further on marks the half-way point for the Yoredale Way and if you feel like celebrating, there is the appropriately positioned Cover Bridge Inn just across the river. Past the pub, take the path on the left across the fields to the banks of the River Cover. Now the way heads north-west, making for the ruins of twelfth-century Middleham Castle.

The castle, administered by English Heritage, is open daily. For a time it was 'the Windsor of the North' while it belonged to the Nevilles and their successors. Lady Anne Neville, daughter of Warwick, the Kingmaker, married Richard III, who acquired the castle. Their son Edward, Prince of Wales, was born here. In those days Middleham had great importance and its keep is one of the largest in England. Middleham itself is a pleasant little town, standing in the shadow of the castle. Famous as a centre for racehorse training, it was once the capital of Wensleydale. The two main squares are lined by solid Georgian houses and snug-looking cottages of local stone.

Visit the parish church and proceed on your way. Beyond several stiles, the route joins the road to Leyburn. Middleham suspension bridge carries traffic over the Ure, but this is no ordinary structure. Somewhat ostentatious in design and looking almost like something from a child's toy cupboard, the

suspension bridge is supported by embattled towers and is rather narrow, so be careful of passing traffic here. Ahead of you there is a steepish climb up to Leyburn, but the rigours of this stretch are amply rewarded by delightful views westwards across Wensleydale.

The town of Leyburn is hardly picturesque but its lofty setting, 700 feet (212 m) above sea level, is a sheer delight. There is an air of calm and a sense of prosperity, particularly on market days. The typically wide marketplace has The Bolton Arms at one end and the parish church at the other, with the usual string of shops, inns and hotels in between.

Leaving the town, make for the Leyburn Shawl, a delightful path signposted near The Bolton Arms. Almost at once you are on the Shawl, a rocky tree-clad ridge providing fine views

The distant but distinctive summit of Pen Hill. The views across the hill and the broad green sweep of Wensleydale are particularly memorable from the Leyburn Shawl, a 2-mile (1.5–km) terrace walk.

across Wensleydale. Pen Hill dominates this corner of the Yorkshire Dales, its distinctive smooth-topped saddle reaching skyward. The route eventually negotiates the slopes of Pen Hill, giving you at this stage some hint of what is in store.

Leyburn Shawl is where Mary Queen of Scots was recaptured two hours after her escape from nearby Bolton Castle in 1568. Some say she dropped her shawl here while fleeing and hence the name given to this path. The Shawl follows a more or less straight line between rows of oaks, evergreens and sycamores but with a sharp precipice dropping away on the left. The scene on the right is unsightly and incongruous by comparison, as you are looking here over stone-quarrying works. At length the path begins to drop down through fields following the waymarker arrows to Tulliscote Farm. Pass a burbling beck and then across several roads and a railway line between them.

Now the way skirts the grounds of Bolton Hall, with its imposing entrance at the heart of Wensley, a village with plenty of pretty grey-stone cottages on view in the main street. The Ure is wide and deep at this point, the river drifting under the arches of its splendid medieval bridge. The village has given its name to Wensleydale, the largest and perhaps finest of all the Yorkshire Dales. There is a tragic side to Wensley, however. In the middle of the sixteenth century a deadly plague devastated what was then a prosperous market town and the place was never really the same again, shrinking in size to the village you see today.

The next stage of the walk is through woodland along a path between the river on the right and the road over on the left. Across the Ure are glimpses of Bolton Hall as the way crosses the Yorkshire Dales National Park boundary just before West Witton. There are several inns in the main street at West Witton, including The Wensleydale Heifer and The Fox and Hounds. Once a mining community, the village has many fine houses cowering in the shadow of Pen Hill, hard by it to the south.

West Witton to Hawes
19 miles (30 km)

Climb steeply away from the village along narrow walled lanes and farm tracks as the route heads west along the craggy northern flanks of Pen Hill towards West Burton. This stretch provides constant, uninterrupted views right across Wensleydale, with its vast patchwork of fields and broad-leaved trees stretching into the distance. The way follows packhorse routes and old drovers' roads with sheep and the occasional hiker for company before descending sharply to the old packhorse bridge at West Burton. As you approach the village, the huge outline of fourteenth-century Bolton Castle is clearly visible over at Redmire on the northern slopes of Wensleydale.

The falls at West Burton are an unexpected delight. Hidden in a secret corner of the village the waters of Walden Beck cascade through this lovely wooded setting of overhanging cliffs and trees, yet just feet away over the packhorse bridge the solid grey-stone houses of West Burton sit like guardians along either side of the elongated village green. The Victorian Spire Cross stands on the green, where the smithy worked and an inn brought together grateful villagers until the early part of this century. The Fox and Hounds can still attempt to quench your thirst however, standing invitingly on the edge of the green.

The way is now across fields beside the Bishopdale Beck. There are several steep climbs before you reach the main A684 road at Aysgarth. Turn left and then right down to the parish church of St Andrew near the river. Aysgarth is a popular place but it is not so much the village that people come to see as the impressive series of falls rushing headlong over the Ure for something like ½ mile (0.8 km) and best seen after a spell of heavy rain. The falls are considered to be one of Yorkshire's best assets and, indeed, they provide a very pretty picture in their well-wooded setting. But the effects of commercialism are instantly recognizable. The roads have yellow lines, there is a fee-paying car park, a café and gift shop and many other attractions to catch the eye of the visiting tourist.

Over the bridge the way follows a route running roughly parallel with the Ure for about 4 miles (6 km). At Nappa Hall, leave the river and head up into the main street of Askrigg. As a town it is first class – quiet, cosy and intimate. Its long, curving street of sturdy, tightly packed houses runs down to the cobbled market square and the parish church of St Oswald beyond. Opposite the church is Skeldale House, familiar to viewers of the television series *All Creatures Great and Small* as James Herriot's veterinary surgery. In reality the surgery is miles away in Thirsk, but Askrigg – probably better known to fans of the stories as the fictional Darrowby – plays host to the location shooting.

Askrigg was once renowned as a centre for clockmaking, with three clockmakers operating at the same time. As the chief market town in Upper Wensleydale, it used to have two annual fairs, for which Queen Elizabeth granted a charter in the sixteenth century.

From St Oswald's follow the signs for Mill Gill Force and after leaving the town, walk along a path high above a delightful wooded ravine with the river murmuring distantly below until, at the end of the path, you reach Mill Gill Force, buried in a leafy hollow of rocks and overhanging trees. Mill Gill Force is a beautiful spot – romantic, moody and

Aysgarth Falls, where the Ure plunges into a delightful gorge and descends 200 feet (61 m) in spectacular fashion over a series of rocky shelves. The falls are best appreciated when the river is in flood. Violets and primroses flower here in abundance during the spring.

mysterious. Few superlatives can adequately describe it. Unquestionably it has to be seen and a visit here lingers long in the memory.

From Mill Gill Force turn back along the path for a short while and then bear right through the gap in the wall. Superb views of Addlebrough Hill dominate the southerly horizon for much of this stretch of the walk. The Romans picked this hill, 1,564 feet (474 m) above sea level, as the site for a look-out

Time has thankfully passed Mill Gill Force by and it is surely the same now as it was in Victorian times, when young ladies walked here in groups from the town, the botanists among them admiring the plants and wild flowers and the water tumbling freely over the rocks. Some no doubt came with their young suitors, as this was a place where young love could blossom, secret and undisturbed. Gazing at the waterfall and its surroundings, it is easy to conjure up images of those precious times, for there is still about Mill Gill Force a strong sense of the past.

The majestic bulk of Addlebrough Hill. Immediately to the south of Skell Gill, a tiny collection of isolated cottages, there is a glorious view of the hill. The Romans chose it as the site for a look-out station.

station. It seems an obvious choice as there would be little to threaten them in such a lofty position. Across the fields is a narrow country road leading to Skell Gill – a name typical of these parts – the place little more than a modest gathering of farm cottages, seemingly in the middle of nowhere. At the end of the track, beyond Skell Gill, the way cuts across fields through tiny openings in an endless series of drystone walls. After some distance the route passes Cote Farm.

Arriving in the tiny village of Sedbusk the way begins to head south-west now, down through peaceful meadows beside the Ure. The route joins forces with Britain's premier long-distance path, the Pennine Way, at this stage and heads for Hawes along a narrow paved path. It is a quaint old town, with much to benefit and interest the walker. There are outdoor shops, hotels and guesthouses, camp and caravan sites, a youth hostel and, perhaps most important of all, plenty of fine scenery on its doorstep. This makes Hawes an ideal base for exploring the Pennines. It is quite a busy place, but thankfully many of its visitors come here on foot to rest for a while – tough, determined hikers meeting the challenge of the Pennine Way.

The Upper Dales Folk Museum at Hawes is worth a visit, giving a fascinating insight into the Dales way of life, its people, trades and customs.

Hawes to Kirkby Stephen
21 miles (34 km)

The final leg of the walk begins about a mile outside Hawes at Hardraw. To reach it, retrace your steps from the town along the road over the river bridge and then as far as the Pennine Way signpost on the left. Join the path and follow it to Hardraw. The village can offer a choice of refreshments. Apart from the Green Dragon Inn, there is the Carthorse Tea Room, where ice cream and sustaining slices of Kendal mint cake are sold.

At the end of the path, behind the inn, a slender waterfall, nearly 100 feet (30 m) high, plunges spectacularly over a limestone ledge into a natural amphitheatre. This is Hardraw Force and the detour is well worthwhile.

Returning to the path, follow the Pennine Way sign and begin the first steep climb of the day. It would not be unusual to find yourself battered by icy winds and rain on this exposed moorland stretch. This is the cruel world of the Pennines and the weather here is often changeable and erratic. The views are stunning – north towards Shunner Fell and the Buttertubs, and all around you the wild summits, the high, green breathtaking fells of Yorkshire, that make the last few miles of this walk so dramatic and so rewarding.

The way skirts the western flanks of Shunner Fell, 2,340 feet (709 m) above sea level, dropping down to Cotterdale, a tiny, hidden collection of cottages beside a tumbling beck. Returning to the high ground once more, there are glorious views from the slopes of Garsdale over a stretch of the scenic Settle–Carlisle railway line. For a while during the late 1980s the future of this line was in grave doubt, when it seemed British Rail would close it because of soaring maintenance costs. Thankfully, the railway was saved, but only at the eleventh hour after a long and arduous battle. The affection in which the Settle–Carlisle railway is held was never more admirably demonstrated than during this critical period. From time to time tourists and train spotters can be seen gathering down at the roadside and even hikers on the path itself eagerly await the unsurpassed spectacle of an approaching steam train, its arrival heralded by the

Hardraw Force, at the end of a long, dank ravine, is reputed to be England's highest unbroken waterfall. The setting is spectacular, with the water plunging over the rocks in a narrow torrent. It is possible to walk underneath the waterfall and yet remain quite dry.

Garsdale, set amid the savage Pennines. For the final leg of the walk, the famous Settle–Carlisle railway line runs parallel with the Yoredale Way, crossing the northern boundary of the Yorkshire Dales National Park.

nostalgic sound of a whistle echoing across the hills and the sight of a distant puff of smoke.

On with the walk again, and along this stretch many weathered old byres can be seen dotted about the hillsides. At this stage you can deviate from the route in order to climb up to Ure Head and the source of the River Ure. It is a lovely spot, just a trickling stream here in its infancy before it grows in strength to eventual maturity on its way to meet the Ouse near York.

The path rejoins the main route at Hell Gill, a deep limestone gorge so wild and sinister in both atmosphere and appearance that it is very aptly named. Indeed, the place belongs in these rugged, untamed surroundings.

Teas and hot, fortifying soup await you at the cottage down by the road. After a cold day spent striding about the Pennines, this break is thoroughly recommended. Hell Gill, incidentally signifies the boundary between Yorkshire and Cumbria and the beck here is the source of the Eden.

Back among the hills the path continues westwards and eventually joins the road. Crossing the road, the way soon leaves it again to follow the banks of the River Eden, passing near to the remains of Pendragon Castle. Local legend suggests that the castle was built by King Arthur's father. Later it passed to the Clifford family.

Beyond it the way presses on along the floor of this delightful valley to reach another ruin, Lammerside Castle. Pass by Wharton Hall, seat of the Wharton family, who founded the local grammar school, and soon, along the wooded banks of the Eden, Kirkby Stephen comes into view. Near a waterfall the route coincides briefly with the B6259 road and then cuts diagonally across the fields to join a main road on the outskirts of this bustling little market town. Kirkby Stephen is closely associated with wool and among its historic old buildings is the thirteenth-century church of St Stephen, which contains ancient carvings and several memorials commemorating the Wharton and Musgrave families.

The Yoredale Way finishes in the centre of Kirkby Stephen, where accommodation is available.

BIBLIOGRAPHY
The Yoredale Way, by J. K. E. Piggin, published by Dalesman, includes directions, maps and photographs, and is available from:
    Dalesman
    Clapham via Lancaster
    North Yorkshire LA2 8EB
or from:
    J. K. E. Piggin
    12 Sussex Close
    Badger Hill
    York YO1 5HY

6 The Wear Valley Way

The Wear Valley Way is a tough, strenuous hike through spectacular North Pennine scenery. This was once the world's major lead-producing area and now the landscape is littered with the remains of long-abandoned mine shafts and disused railway lines. Weardale has everything for the keen walker: scenic bursts of forest and woodland and bleak expanses of empty moorland and hillside. But there are gentler alternatives as well, including pleasant villages and some pretty stretches beside the River Wear.

The Wear Valley Way was the brainchild of Alan Earnshaw, who, after moving to the north-east of England, was initially sceptical about the potential for such a walk in this part of Durham. However, as he explored in the wilds of Weardale, he recognized the possibilities for a long-distance path and subsequently began to devote much of his time to route-planning, reconnaissance and seeking local-authority approval. At length his efforts paid off and the way was officially opened in the summer of 1979.

The walk begins at the Killhope Wheel picnic area, high up in the Weardale Forest. Near to the start is the Lead-mining Centre, a museum illustrating in a most interesting and informative way how the industry operated for centuries in this area. All the lead mines were closed by the early part of the twentieth century, although 100 years ago you could not travel very far without spotting a huge water wheel similar to the giant contraption at Killhope.

From the picnic area the way weaves around the slopes of Weardale through the villages of Cowshill and Rookhope, where the file on a bizarre murder mystery nearly 200 years ago still remains open, and on to Frosterley.

Beyond this village the path climbs across Pikestone Fell and then makes for Hamsterley Forest, an oasis of trees and peaceful riverside clearings on the doorstep of Durham's industrial heartland. The walk passes through the grounds of

Length 46 miles (73 km)
Start Killhope Wheel near Stanhope
Finish Willington
Going Tough in places
Ordnance Survey Maps 87, 92, 93
Waymarking Arrows and standard waymarkers. A compass is recommended for moorland areas

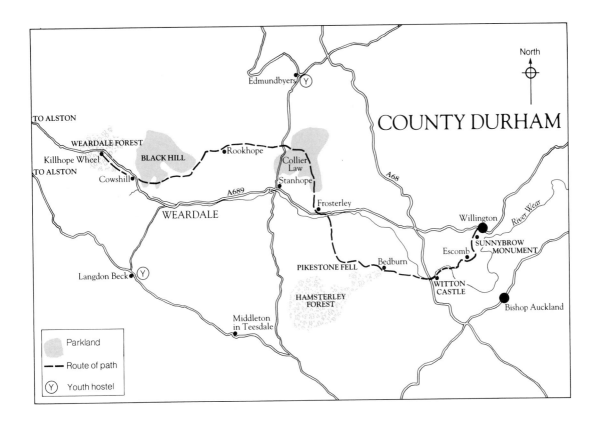

Witton Castle, unusually the setting for a camp and caravan park. After a visit to the Saxon church at Escomb, the way runs past the Miners' Monument at Sunnybrow. It is in the shape of an old colliery tub, mounted on a simple base, and signifies a bitter, historic struggle in the mid-nineteenth century between miners, union bosses and colliery management.

The Wear Valley Way finishes just beyond the monument on the outskirts of Willington.

Accommodation is available in some of the villages along the route and there are several youth hostels quite close to the start of the walk at Alston and Langdon Beck. Buses serve Killhope Wheel and Willington.

Killhope Wheel to Rookhope
12 miles (19 km)

The walk starts at the Killhope Wheel picnic area, close to the well-designed Lead-mining Centre. Surrounded by dense forest and grouse moors, the site includes an expanded display on the life of the lead miner and his family. Among many other attractions are the giant restored water wheel which powered

Killhope Wheel Lead-mining Centre. Extensive restoration has taken place here in recent times and now the Lead-mining Centre has much to interest the visitor. The overshot water wheel which powered the crushing mill is one of the site's greatest attractions.

the crushing machinery and the mine 'shop', where miners slept sometimes four to a bed during their working week. There are also working models, refreshments and a gift shop.

Begin by walking along the main A689 road for a short distance towards Killhope Cross. Leave the road at a footpath sign, cross the Killhope Burn and enter the Weardale Forest. The path skirts the top of Kidd's Dam and then runs on to Cowhorse Hush. ('Hush' was a term used in lead-mining which meant to separate lead from earth by the application of water; the name came from the sound of water made as it escaped from the earth dams above and poured down over the soil and vegetation in its path.)

A little beyond the Hush the way joins a forest ride. Follow it until it joins the road leading to Wellhope Farm. Then turn left and walk down the lane to the point where the Killhope and Wellhope Burns meet. As you approach the river you will see a road swinging back to the right. Take the road and then the track by the treatment and control station, following it to a farm, Blakey Field. The way presses on to the ruins of High Rush Farm and then follows paths and farm tracks to the neighbouring farm of Low Rush.

From here the route is across fields, passing several more farms to join a track climbing steeply to the junction with the main A689 road. Turn right here and head towards Cowshill. This is a pretty village with an assortment of old houses and cottages clinging to the hillsides, a hotel and shop at its centre, a sturdy stone road bridge and the charming Sedling Burn tumbling down from the fells.

The next stage of the walk begins by heading north-east out of the village, past old mine workings and disused shafts. Following the bridleway, here and there it is worth pausing during the ascent to drink in the splendid Pennine views. Skirt the lower slopes of Black Hill, heading east over Sedling Rake, at nearly 2.000 feet (606 m) the highest point on the walk. Soon the way skirts a young plantation on the right of the track and then joins the road at Middlehope Top. A spell on the road Middlehope Bank. Here the road disappears almost vertically down a steep bank. The way traverses the far moorland slopes towards Scarsike Head.

Cowshill. The Sedling Burn dashes down to this pretty hillside village set amid rugged moors and fells. Not far away is the point at which three counties – Durham, Cumbria and Northumberland – meet.

follows, though it hardly spoils the enjoyment of the walk. It is quite conceivable that you will not see any traffic at all along this stretch of road, for it is a narrow, isolated single-track strip running for some distance in a straight line, bordered by drystone walls and fences.

The surroundings here are suitably wild and windswept. One or two buildings are visible in the distance but mainly it is an empty, desolate landscape of distant valleys and, nearer at hand, high, sweeping fells divided into haphazard squares and rectangles by a network of drystone walls. The road drops down rapidly to reach Middlehope Burn and then climbs again towards Scarsike Head. On arriving at the junction turn right and head south in the direction of Westgate. After about ½ mile (0.8 km) the way turns left and follows a walled track, Red Road, leading eventually out on to open moorland. The route is rather vague and uncertain beyond the track but you should be heading north-east towards Greenmere Head.

Soon the way drops down over Smailsburn Common to the old lead miners' dam. Beyond it the route keeps to a track crossing the Rookhope Burn and then very quickly reaches the road. Turn right and follow the road into the village of Rookhope, a compact community with a shop and The Rookhope Inn at its centre. Again some of the homes climb up the surrounding hillsides and here and there long lines of little terraced houses serve as a reminder of the days when the village was an important lead-mining centre in the North Pennine Orefield.

Rookhope to Hamsterley Forest
22 miles (35 km)

From the centre of Rookhope the way heads up a stony track to reach a Y-shaped fork. Bear left here and follow the old disused railway incline towards Parkhead. The old line was, at almost 1,700 feet (515 m) the highest standard-gauge railway ever built in Britain. Its purpose was to transport ore but by the turn of the century there was very little demand for it. After that it fulfilled various roles – one of them being to carry shooting parties in search of grouse.

The route passes the ruins of Redgate Head and continues relentlessly across this bleak, lonely landscape. A little later the path drops below the military transmitter mast at Horseshoe Hill and joins the B6278 road. There is a youth hostel about 3 miles (4.5 km) north of here in the village of Edmundbyers.

Follow the road for a brief spell and then head up towards the police radio masts on Collier Law. On reaching the mast, turn right and head downhill over East Collier Law Moss. Fatherley Hill is your next objective. Beyond it follow the road down to a junction and then bear right and join the A689.

There is nothing particularly remarkable or unusual about Rookhope save for the curious, unsolved mystery of the Redburn Skulls – a story that is as dark and full of foreboding as the savage Pennine hills encircling this village.

It was in 1918 that a number of skulls, nine in all, were found by a group of workmen toiling in a quarry near Redburn Mine outside Rookhope. The skulls lay in a shallow grave, eight of them undamaged and intact, the ninth clearly having been dealt several severe blows. No other human remains were discovered but in the eye sockets of the skulls a number of bronze coins were found, including a cartwheel penny of 1799. Though it was customary to cover the eyes of the dead with coins, there is no logical explanation as to why this site was chosen to bury nine skulls . . . other than murder.

It is indeed a grisly tale, all the more fascinating because of the lack of clues. Who were the victims? Why were they murdered? And by whom? These are questions that will probably never be answered.

The way turns left here and enters Frosterley. The winding main street is lined by houses and shops and beyond them, at the far end of the village, The Frosterley Inn. A narrow stone track leads off the street and down to the parish church of St Michael, built in the 1860s. Access is restricted, reflecting the lack of planning here. The church, hidden away from the main part of the village, almost seems an afterthought. The village is famous for Frosterley marble, a grey limestone filled with fossils which turns black when polished. There is a memorial in the church to Frosterley marble which refers to it adorning churches and cathedrals throughout the world.

South of the village the way crosses the River Wear by a footbridge. The next section of the walk is over farm tracks and roads used as public paths as the way approaches the edge of Pikestone Fell. Climb steeply up through the fields towards the fell. Once there, keep an eye out for the various cairns common to this area and originally intended to help miners locate fell-top mines. The path now makes for an old farm and then crosses South Grain Beck before reaching Hamsterley Forest. Once there, the way keeps to forest roads and tracks, making for the remains of Metcalf's House, an old coaching inn.

There is an alternative, drier route between Pikestone Fell and Metcalf's House. The path, indistinct at times, runs

St Michael's church, Frosterley, which houses an example of the famous Frosterley marble that has been quarried in the locality for centuries. According to the tribute in the church, 'This Frosterley marble and limestone adorns cathedrals and churches throughout the world.'

between the cairns and over heather moorland to a place called Doctor's Gate. From here a track leads to Metcalf's House. The walk then follows a track on the north bank of the Ayhope Beck, eventually coming upon the forest drive. Here turn left and follow the drive as far as the Forestry Commission Information Centre and offices.

There are many facilities for visitors within the forest, including picnic areas with tables and benches, pony trekking, waymarked nature trails and a number of delightful scenic forest drives. Among the various conifer trees found here are Scots pine, sitka spruce, Japanese larch and western red cedar. There are also many species of broad-leaved trees, including wild cherry, alder, sycamore, wych-elm and hawthorn.

Hamsterley Forest to Willington

12 miles (19 km)

Leaving this south-east corner of the forest, the way heads along a pretty stretch of the Bedburn Beck. The hamlet of Bedburn is really just a house or two, with the beck hurrying down among the trees below the bridge. But it is a pretty setting none the less and worth pausing for a few moments to admire.

Resuming the Wear Valley Way, the walk now traces a route roughly parallel with the Bedburn Beck as it snakes through the countryside over on the left. Beyond Howlea Bridge the way passes Snape Gate Farm. Avoid the track crossing the beck and continue along the south bank to Park House Farm, near where the Bedburn joins the River Wear. Keeping to the clear track, pass several more farms before reaching the road at Diddridge Crossroads. The way turns left here and follows the road for nearly a mile, until the junction with the A68 at the bottom of Crakehill Bank.

On the opposite side of the road a path goes up a sharp bank and then runs alongside the Wear, emerging at the roadside by the entrance to Witton Castle. The river is quite wide at this

Hamsterley Forest – the largest area of woodland in Durham. Bought by the Forestry Commission in 1927, the 5,000-acre (12,355-ha) forest is a paradise for walkers and naturalists. There are numerous paths and rides, and among other creatures roe deer and red squirrels may be glimpsed amid the trees.

point, its banks thick with trees. The village of Witton-le-Wear is a short walk from here and boasts a pub.

Pass into the grounds of Witton Castle, following the way as it heads along a drive through the estate. Often the place is alive with the activity of holiday-makers and other visitors and caravans seem to appear at every turn.

The way runs alongside Witton Row Beck and past the ruins of Holme House. At this point it crosses the beck and follows the right bank of the Wear. On the far side of the river Witton Nature Reserve and Bird Sanctuary soon become visible. Before long the way joins a track running to the road. On reaching it, turn right and head for Witton Park Village. Then follow a route running between the railway and the river. The path is partly across fields and meadows as far as the former pit village of Escomb.

The road circles the Saxon church of St John the Evangelist and not surprisingly across the way there is The Saxon Inn for those desirous of a drink and something to eat perhaps. The precise age of the church is unknown, but it is believed to date from the seventh century. For a time during the nineteenth century it lay dormant and neglected, but an appeal was later launched and it was eventually restored. The stones used in its reconstruction come from the nearby Roman fort at Binchester.

The Rocking Strike came about as a result of bitter disagreement over productivity in the mines. The trouble began when mine managers demanded impossibly high tub loads from the miners. The newly established Miners' Association called the men out on strike, while the mine bosses immediately ordered the arrest of its leaders. The union, however, appointed a solicitor to act for them and his efforts on their behalf led to the twelve men concerned being released from Durham jail. Bitter, angry but still undefeated, the mine owners then ordered the eviction of the miners and their families from their homes. A savage and violent struggle ensued between the miners and the bailiffs, who brought in groups of hired thugs to help them. The battle ended in a victory for the bailiffs. The miners and their families, now homeless, fled for shelter to a primitive stockade beside the Durham railway. It was a pitiful sight. Because of what happened many never worked again. However, something good eventually came of the whole sad business. Parliament intervened and miners were subsequently allowed to elect their own chosen representatives to check the colliery tubs at the bank top.

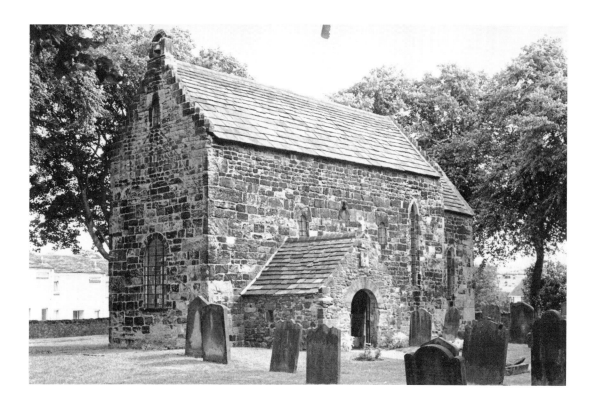

On leaving the church, take the road in the direction of the Wear and on reaching the river turn right and proceed along the south bank through a copse and then beside a meadow. Cross over a stream and follow the track up through the trees towards the top of Broken Bank and the railway line. From here it is a short walk to the road and the picnic site at West Mills.

Next is a brief stretch on the A689 road, followed by a mile or so along the rather grandly named Bishop Brandon Walkway. This, in fact, is the name now given to the old Durham–Bishop Auckland railway. In a while the path reaches the remains of Hunwick Station, where fortunately there is a pub, The New Monkey. Suitably refreshed for the last couple of miles, return to the old railway line and continue in the same direction as before. When you reach a footpath crossing the old track, turn right and drop down to the fields below.

The way passes over a stream and then enters a wood before joining a farm track running along the river bank. Cross the Holy Well Burn and then make a short detour to look at the Sunnybrow Monument, possibly having a drink at The Brown Trout Inn just across the road. The monument stands by itself on an open playing field, overlooked by rows of terraced houses and bungalows. The inscription reads: 'Erected to

St John the Evangelist, Escomb. Surrounded by houses, this is one of the most complete Anglo-Saxon churches in England. Its exact age is not known but it is reputed to date back to the seventh century.

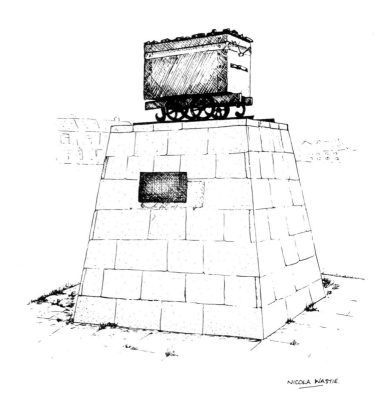

NICOLA WASTIE.

The Sunnybrow Monument, erected in memory of the Rocking Strike of 1863.

commemorate Rocking Strike of 1863 which was the forerunner of the Checkweigh system in the collieries of County Durham and in memory of the men and boys killed in the mines of Sunnybrow, Brancepeth and Oakenshaw – unveiled 19th March, 1976 by J. Gormley, O.B.E., President of the National Union of Mineworkers'.

Return to the main path and cross the footbridge. The way then follows the riverside path, the water now on your left. Very soon the path reaches the picnic site at Jubilee Bridge on the outskirts of Willington, where the walk ends. The town has plenty of shops and a number of public houses in its main streets for those wishing to rest for a while and celebrate the finish of the walk.

BIBLIOGRAPHY
The Wear Valley Way, by Alan Earnshaw, published by Discovery Guides, includes maps, sketches and directions, and is available from the publisher. Write to:
1 Market Place
Middleton-in-Teesdale
Teesdale
Durham DL12 0QG
A new edition will be available in due course.

7 The Speyside Way

The second long-distance footpath north of the border to have been officially designated by the Countryside Commission for Scotland and formally opened in 1981, the Speyside Way is not simply a pleasant exercise in river-bank walking. Much of the route is along the valley of this famous salmon and whisky river, but away from the swiftly flowing Spey there are exhilarating forays into thickly wooded high country and over rolling heather moorland and bog with distant hills and mountains stretching to the horizon.

The Spey, so well loved by fly fishermen, rises in the Corrieyairack Forest, over 100 miles (160 km) to the south-west. Walking along its banks it is easy to spot the prized salmon that make the trip from the North Atlantic to their native river to spawn. Beginning the walk beside the Moray Firth, you will be filled with a sense of having journeyed as well. Spey Bay is one of the most northerly outposts of the British Isles and, appropriately, the place has an air of bleak isolation about it. From here the path follows the river inland to Fochabers. South of the town, it climbs on to higher ground between rows of larch, Scots pine, birch and spruce before reaching the village of Craigellachie, where there is an interesting visitors' centre, which houses the headquarters of the Speyside Way Ranger Service, and a graceful nineteenth-century bridge over the river, built by Thomas Telford.

The village marks the start of a lengthy stretch along the old disused Strathspey railway line, providing flat, easy walking beside or near the Spey as far as Ballindalloch. The Speyside Way offers a welcome distraction during this stage as it follows part of the famous 70-mile (112-km) Malt Whisky Trail, stumbling upon several distilleries directly beside the path. One of which, Tamdhu, is open to the public and offers a guided tour, a visitors' centre and, as you leave, the opportunity to sample a wee dram!

Originally, the path finished at the old Ballindalloch Station,

Length 45 miles (72 km)
Start Spey Bay
Finish Tomintoul
Going Mainly level walking with some steep climbs midway and in latter stages
Ordnance Survey Maps 28, 36
Waymarking Wooden posts bearing the symbol of a thistle within a hexagon; a compass may be needed during the final moorland stretch

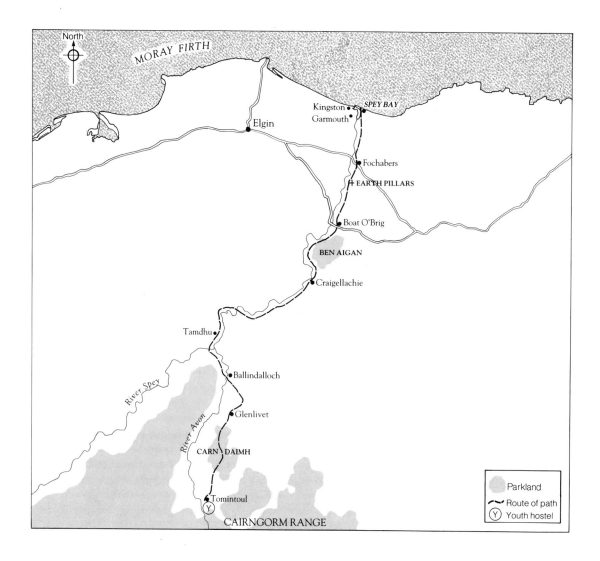

but a 15-mile (24-km) spur, officially opened in June 1988, now provides by far the most spectacular scenery of the entire walk. With magnificent, breathtaking views of the snow-covered Cairngorm peaks in the distance, the high-level route leaves the Spey far behind it by following old drovers' roads and cart tracks to the windswept summit of Carn Daimh and then down again to Tomintoul, which at 1,100 feet (333 m) is the highest village in the Highlands.

Although there are some isolated stretches, walkers should easily reach accommodation by nightfall. A limited bus service operates between Spey Bay and Tomintoul during the summer months. The nearest town to the start of the walk is Elgin, which is on the mainline railway for Aberdeen and Inverness.

Spey Bay to Craigellachie
17 miles (27 km)

Spey Bay is little more than a row of stone-built houses and bungalows overlooking the Moray Firth, with a hotel and golf course at one end and the estuary of the River Spey at the other. On the far bank there are glimpses of Kingston and Garmouth, two neighbouring villages.

A short distance from the start of the Speyside Way is the old, restored Tugnet Ice House, hard by the pebble beach. It has a permanent exhibition illustrating the history and background of the salmon industry and commercial fishing on the river. Looking not unlike a collection of stone Anderson shelters, the Ice House, built in 1830 and thought to be one of the largest in Scotland, was last in use in the late 1960s. It was here, in the days before refrigeration, that salmon was stored prior to being sold.

The path is clearly waymarked and begins by following the eastern bank of the river as it flows and eddies between shingle spits and margins of thick undergrowth. The river and its estuary are a haven for birdlife – shelducks, waders, oyster catchers and curlews are among the various species inhabiting this part of the coastline.

Heading upriver, this is flat, gentle walking over level fishermen's paths and stony tracks. Passing a footpath sign to Garmouth via the Spey Viaduct – part of the former Elgin–Aberdeen coast railway – the way skirts open fields for some time, with bursts of dense, dark woodland on the right screening the river. Briefly, the path leaves the flat fields and cuts between verges of gorse scrubland and wild flowers. The Spey is not visible here, though its fast-flowing water is within earshot as you make your way along the track. Those looking in vain for glimpses of the river are soon rewarded, however, as suddenly the path rises steeply and stumbles upon it. On this stretch of the Spey, there are glorious clear views both upstream and down.

It is usually quiet and uneventful here, but there was an occasion when the river was called upon to fulfil a vital role in the aftermath of an epic disaster. After the Great Fire of London pipes made from timber for a new drainage system were floated downstream and shipped from Garmouth. Years later, during the last war, many of those old pipes were discovered, still intact, amid the debris of the bombed capital.

The path courts the river for some distance now, running in the main a little above it. There are several scenic reaches before the way leaves the river bank and joins the road from Spey Bay, crossing through semi-wooded countryside, much of which is parkland belonging to the Gordon Castle Estate at Fochabers.

River sunlight and shadows. The Spey is renowned as a favourite haunt of salmon anglers. The salmon scent the river out in Spey Bay and are then drawn instinctively 100 miles (160 km) upstream in search of their spawning grounds.

Just below the road junction with the A96, the way rejoins the river path and passes under several road bridges before entering woodland again beside the Spey. Soon it leaves the river and follows the banks of the Burn of Fochabers. The surroundings here are congested, enclosed by trees and private gardens as the path skirts the residential outskirts of Fochabers. A short walk from here brings you into the centre of the village, where The Gordon Arms Hotel and a good range of bed and breakfast accommodation can supply your needs.

Fochabers dates mainly from the eighteenth century and was designed to a grid-iron pattern. It has a rich assortment of buildings, including the elegantly fashioned Milne's High School and the Bellie parish church. At one end of the village high street is the grand entrance to Gordon Castle, once the seat of the Duke of Richmond and Gordon. Just before the Second World War, however, the estate was sold to the Crown and the great building was subsequently demolished.

The way heads south out of Fochabers beside a school and then out into open countryside again, cutting along paths between fields and through peaceful, undiscovered woodland and bracken. Climbing into higher country now, there are good, far-reaching views over wooded landscapes that have more than a hint of Scandinavian appearance about them. The views are constant as the way follows a narrow country lane for some time, with frequent backward glimpses of the winding Spey as it heads for the sea. So far the route of the

Lower Spey Valley. A Scandinavian landscape of lush fields and woodland through which meanders the Spey. These wide valleys are known in the Highlands as straths.

journey has acted as its faithful close companion. Beyond the river, and merging almost imperceptibly with the skyline, is the vast expanse of the Moray Firth, while nearer at hand, down below through the fields, there are further signs of the Spey, with its familiar shingle banks visible between the trees.

The road heads for Aultderg, part of the Speymouth Forest, where there are a Forestry Commission car park, picnic tables and benches and a splendid terraced path above steep wooded slopes leading through the pine trees to a spectacular gorge on the east bank of the Spey. Here lie the Earth Pillars, which are rain-eroded pinnacles of red sandstone overlooking the river.

The path runs down to a delightful viewpoint where there are seats and magnificent panoramic views of the Spey Valley, with the river below meandering lazily towards distant, rolling hills. Back on the road the route heads south again, dropping into a wooded glen and then rising steeply on the other side, with further views back towards the coastline at Spey Bay. In front of you is a gradual climb up through the fields as the Speyside Way makes deeper inroads into the pleasant open countryside and wooded scenery of Moray.

The road winds up and down rather monotonously and after some time begins a steady descent through the woodlands of Delfur Lodge, zigzagging down to the road and railway bridges at Boat O'Brig. Before the present structures were built, a ferry boat – the *Boat O'Brig* or 'Boat over the Bridge' – crossed the river at this point. Prior to that there had been another bridge, probably medieval in date, here but it fell into disrepair some time after the Reformation.

On the opposite side of the road the way makes for a track up towards Bridgeton Farm and the afforested slopes of Knock More and Ben Aigan. It is a gentle pull at first, becoming progressively steeper as it makes for the trees. This stretch of the walk is physically one of the most strenuous, with the path following a gradual ascending spiral over Forestry Commission tracks. Eventually, though, you get a glorious high-level view northwards over the trees and back across the lower Spey Valley towards the coast. All the recognizable features of the landscape are here, including the road and rail bridges at Boat O'Brig and distant reaches of the winding river as it begins to skirt the base of Ben Aigan.

The track, keeping below the 1,544-feet (468-m) summit, winds on interminably through the forest, where the surroundings seem hardly to alter at all. Here and there comparisons can be drawn with the Coed Morgannwg Way in south Wales (Chapter 11), for the landscape is much the same. With long, endless stretches of forest track and repetitious glimpses of a distant valley or hillside, there seems little prospect of a significant change in the nature of the scenery. Then, at last, the Speyside Way begins a gradual downward gradient and ultimately joins the road. The route now follows a pleasantly wooded lane for 2 miles (3 km) or so on its approach to Craigellachie.

Notice, on a sharp bend in the road, the splendid, typically Scottish architecture of Arndilly House, with its distinctive turrets and ornate portico. Dating back to the mid-eighteenth century, the building is privately owned but cannot fail to be appreciated by those passing by on the road. The last leg of this section is along the lane through mature beech and alder woodland, with brief glimpses of the Spey over to the right between the trees.

Arriving in Craigellachie, note the Fiddichside Inn on the left, prettily situated, as its name suggests, beside the River Fiddich and only a stone's throw from the spot where it joins the Spey. Turn right at the junction and follow the route of the old disused Strathspey railway line into the village centre. The Speyside Way Visitors' Centre lies on the right of the path at Boat O'Fiddich Cottage, just before the road bridge.

The focal point of Craigellachie is its quiet main street, lined with sturdy-looking houses and shops and several hotels, making it handy for an overnight stop. The village is fundamentally Victorian in both character and appearance. It grew in stature towards the end of the nineteenth century, when the population increased substantially.

Not far from the village centre, tucked away on its own down a quiet side road, is perhaps Craigellachie's most notable attraction, Telford's Bridge. Lonely and redundant – it is now bypassed by a modern road bridge close by – the bridge was designed and built by Thomas Telford in 1814 and restored to its original design in the early 1960s. Supported on castellated granite turrets, it spans the river gracefully, its impressive structure a constant and unchanging testimony to Telford's unique technical ability.

Craigellachie to Ballindalloch
13 miles (21 km)

The Strathspey line was built in 1863 and carried passengers on excursions between Aberdeen and Boat of Garten, to the south-west of Grantown-on-Spey. Though long disused as a railway, the old track has been put to very good use as an integral part of the Speyside Way. At times the path is almost smothered by a thick curtain of foliage along its banks. There seems to be an abundance of rosebay willow herb, with its slender cones of deep pink flowers, and many kinds of moths and butterflies are drawn to the hidden cuttings of dense undergrowth.

From Craigellachie follow the course of the old railway line as it runs parallel with the river south-west to Aberlour. The

Bridge at Craigellachie. Built by Thomas Telford in the early nineteenth century at a cost of £8,000, the slender iron bridge spans 150 feet (45 m) of the Spey below Craigellachie Rock. The road bridge nearby, which eventually replaced it, was opened in 1972.

village soon peeps into view, as does the suspension bridge spanning the river. Aberlour, a popular base for salmon fishing, was founded early in the last century by Charles Grant of Wester Elchies, the local laird. According to popular belief, the first villagers here took stones from the nearby river bed to build their homes – a quaint idea that somehow has a ring of truth about it. The old station yard is now a delightful riverside park, with the former buildings neatly converted into tea rooms and the like. The park is named after Alice Littler, who with her husband ran an orphanage in the village.

South of Aberlour the path continues to follow the route of the old railway, with the river and its regular cluster of fishermen across the fields to your right. It soon enters a semi-wooded section to arrive at Dailuaine Halt. Peering around, it is possible to identify the old disused platform and perhaps picture the little halt as it might have been in the heyday of this railway, years before its decline and eventual closure in the late 1960s. Unlike the thoughtfully planned station conversion at Aberlour, the old halt at Dailuaine remains virtually unchanged, if a little neglected.

Another wooded stretch of old track links Dailuaine with the road before the way crosses the Spey at Carron. The path goes over the road bridge into the village, with the rusting girders of the old railway bridge alongside it on the left.

The sleepy village centre has several guesthouses, an inn and the Imperial Distillery at the end of its main street. After the

NICOLA WASTIE

long stretch of track between here and Aberlour, Carron is ideally placed for those in need of overnight rest and refreshment.

Dailuaine Halt on the disused Strathspey line.

Leaving the peace of the village behind you at last, the way follows the old track again, with impressive, high-level views over the river and the wooded slopes beyond. This is the very heart of malt whisky country and the route directly passes two distilleries in quick succession beside the former track: the first is Knockando, the second Tamdhu, founded in the 1890s here because of its close proximity to the railway line.

The old station here has been imaginatively restored and the newly refurbished buildings now play host to a most interesting visitors' centre, which provides guided tours over the distillery at certain times of the year with a chance to sample the golden liquor afterwards.

The path keeps to the old railway still, offering pleasant river vistas from time to time. It crosses a series of bridges before reaching an impressive railway viaduct, now a listed monument, near Ballindalloch Station.

Ballindalloch to Tomintoul
15 miles (24 km)

The next 2 miles (3 km) or so are along the road but there are some pleasant diversions to compensate. From the old station yard turn left and walk down to the main road. At the junction go left passing, beside the River Avon, the splendid fairytale gatehouse at the entrance to Ballindalloch Castle.

Beyond Ballindalloch turn right near the Delnashaugh Hotel further up the road and keep to the B9008 for about ½ mile (0.8

The castle itself cannot be seen from the road but Ballindalloch is regarded as one of the finest examples of baronial architecture in this part of Scotland. Believed to have been built between 1542 and 1700, the castle witnessed many changes over the years. A favourite legend here suggests that Ballindalloch was originally scheduled to be built further upstream – the higher ground chosen was considered to be more easily defendable – but work on its construction was disrupted by mysterious forces. Builders would arrive at daybreak to find their work of the previous day destroyed in their absence and the laird was dogged by persistent, nagging dreams directing him to build the castle in the cow-haugh or plain near the river. Work was switched to the lower-lying ground and the castle was eventually completed without further disturbance.

Close to this spot the River Avon, pronounced A'an, joins the Spey as it begins to head south-west towards Grantown. From now on the path follows a route parallel with the Avon, a river so extraordinarily translucent as to inspire the following couplet:

The water o'A'an it rins sae clear
Twould beguile a man o'a hunner year.

The river is thought to have been named after Fingal's wife, who was drowned near the source further to the south.

km). There are clear, frequent waymarkers on this stretch. Leaving the road eventually, the route makes for a stone track signposted to Aldich. Passing the guesthouse, the track begins an upward pull towards the Hill of Deskie, turning right some way up on to a rougher track through the heather. This is wild, untamed moorland – a far cry from the earlier gentle river-valley scenery and with few signs to tell you that twentieth-century civilization, for good or bad, is not far away. Only the soft moan of the breeze as it tugs the heather and the sound of occasional birdsong seem to break the acute silence.

The path swings further into the hills, with spectacular views all around. This area is dominated by the Hill of Deskie and the land over which the path crosses is part of Deskie Farm. Over the crest of the hill and down the other side through the heather there is a vast, glorious panorama of hills and moorland sweeps topped by the jagged ridge of the Cairngorm Mountains away on the distant skyline. Even on a sunny day in mid-summer, their peaks are flecked with snow.

Follow the fences and the waymakers as the route descends in winding, somewhat haphazard fashion towards the distant Glenlivet distillery, standing distinctively in a hollow in the hills. The way swings down through open moorland and over field-boundary paths and narrow lanes before reaching the road at Glenlivet. Turning left over the old road bridge the route follows the River Livet for a short distance to cross it by the pedestrian suspension bridge, built in 1983. From here it is a short walk to the road again and the entrance to Minmore House Hotel and Restaurant, home of George Smith, founder of the Glenlivet distillery, who died in 1871.

The road runs straight through the heart of the distillery complex, established in 1824, taking the route of the Speyside Way with it. At the top of the hill there is another hotel, Blairfindy Lodge, the last watering hole before the long, lonely haul to Tomintoul.

Beyond the hotel the way parts from the road and follows an old cinder track up towards the trees. The gentle, protective circle of hills behind prompt you to pause and drink in the splendid views, which surely confirm that this final leg offers a distinctly dramatic edge to the Speyside Way. The view

Visitors' Centre at Tamdhu distillery. This splendid wooden building used to be the railway station. Tamdhu, meaning 'Little Dark Hill' in Gaelic, is one of many distilleries on the Malt Whisky Trail.

southwards is again a rumpled carpet of moorland and high, rugged mountain tops looking towards the Cairngorm range. Here you are in a solitary world of softly swelling hills and uplands, grazing sheep and acre upon acre of forestry plantation.

This is a slow gradual climb through the heather – warm work on a hot summer's day but on the whole fairly undemanding. Passing a sign to Tomnavoulin, the way makes directly for the final ascent to the 1,850-feet (560-m) summit of Carn Daimh – the Hill of the Stags. It is a short but steep climb and the summit is neat and level, having the appearance almost of a platform perched above the hills, exposed to all weathers and with 360-degree views over this spectacular landscape. Undoubtedly, standing here has to make the sometimes wearisome haul to this lonely hill top worth the effort. The views across to the Cairngorm range invite admiration, though looking back towards Glenlivet the scene is only marginally less spectacular.

After this, the final stretch to Tomintoul might seem something of an anticlimax. It is a mostly downhill run, initially beside and then through plantations of pine trees before breaking cover to head across the open expanse of heather moorland and peat bog known as the Feithmusach. The village

Mountain wilderness. From Carn Daimh there are unparalleled views of the Cairngorms to the south – a rugged, immensely beautiful landscape of forest, lochs and high mountain peaks.

Opposite The romantic gatehouse at Ballindalloch Castle. About 1 mile (1.6 km) from here, the path and the river part company at the confluence of the Spey and the Avon.

The Square at Tomintoul – a bracing sort of place where the air is clear and clean and the streets wide and spacious. The local economy is based on tourism, farming and whisky distilling.

of Tomintoul is visible from here, buried in a fold in the hills and dominated by the Cairngorm peaks, rising to over 4,000 feet (1,212 m) above it. Passing alongside further bursts of woodland, the way drops down quite steeply to reach a minor road. Turn left here. At a sharp bend the route leaves the road and heads down to the River Conglass, winding through the fields below. Cross the river by the wooden footbridge and keep to quiet paths and tracks as far as the road. Here the way turns left and after a short distance enters the village of Tomintoul by way of its long main street.

If an overnight stop is on your itinerary, there is much to choose from in the way of accommodation. Hotels and guesthouses line the street and the square beyond. With its bracing air, bustling centre and nearby trout streams, Tomintoul is a popular, pleasant enough setting for the end of the Speyside Way.

BIBLIOGRAPHY
A comprehensive leaflet with a general description of the route, plus sketches, useful information and map is available from:
    Moray District Council
    District Headquarters
    High Street
    Elgin IV30 1BX

8 The Calderdale Way

The narrow Pennine valleys of West Yorkshire are rich in history and industrial heritage. It was the great Industrial Revolution of the nineteenth century that really awakened them and used them to their full advantage. With the coming of steam, grasping mill owners built on vacant, undeveloped tracts of land and soon the whole area was humming with the sounds of working machinery, all brought to life by throngs of industrious Victorians.

Many of the old mills have long gone and some of those remaining are probably heritage museums or the like, but whatever their fate, these great Victorian monstrosities became monuments to a vital turning point in the fortunes of the nation.

The Calderdale Way follows this austere industrial scene, considerably revitalized in places, against a rugged Pennine backdrop and together they are a perfect match. You are never far from a dark satanic mill or a blackened drystone wall, and the names here have a peculiarly northern ring to them: Stoodley Pike, Scout Rock, Crow Hill, Mankinholes, Mytholmroyd, Emley Moor and Hardcastle Crags. To many this is West Yorkshire at its grimy, glorious best.

The area has a strong feeling of history, too. It oozes character from every pore. Away from the old industrial landscapes and wonderfully evocative mill-town scenes in the valleys below, there is an even greater sense of the past. Up on the bleak gritstone fells, the path is often strewn with rocks and stones – according to legend, the work of giants who were given to hurling boulders about the countryside.

Officially opened in 1978, the route winds somewhat precariously along either side of the Calder Valley, taking its name from the Metropolitan Borough of Calderdale, which was established in 1974. With a series of link paths giving access at virtually any point, the way follows ancient packhorse routes and paths between Brighouse, marking the eastern boundary,

Length 50 miles (80 km)
A circular route with a suggested start and finish at Clay House Visitors' Centre, West Vale, Greetland, near Halifax
Going Fairly undemanding but with a few steep, quite strenuous climbs
Ordnance Survey Maps 103, 104, 110
Outdoor Leisure Map 21 – South Pennines
Waymarking Calderdale Way signposts and yellow arrows with C. W. symbols

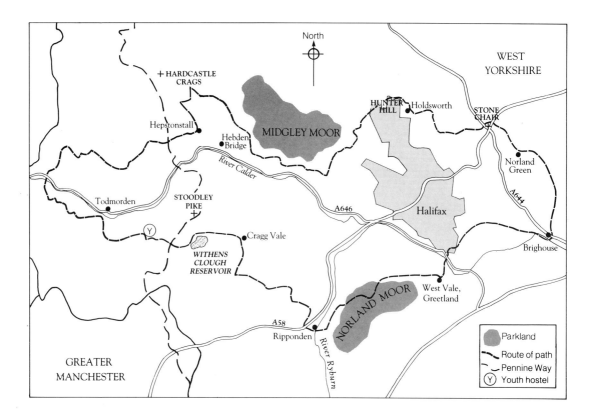

and the town of Todmorden at the western end. Along the southern route, the villages of Ripponden, Mankinholes and Lumbutts are conservation areas, while Withens Clough Reservoir lies in remote Pennine territory, only a stone's throw from the course of the Pennine Way, over which the Calderdale Way passes. To the north the way encounters the picturesque old weavers' village of Heptonstall, delightful Luddenden Dean and the rich, rural calm of the Shibden Valley. The last leg of the Calderdale Way is slightly more industrial, though it hardly intrudes.

Accommodation is generally easy to find and public transport is good, with railway stations at Brighouse and Halifax and buses linking the various towns and villages.

West Vale to Cragg Vale
9 miles (14 km)

The Calderdale Way begins behind the Visitors' Centre at Clay House, West Vale, a seventeenth-century building, illustrating the history of Calderdale and containing the replica of a Roman altar discovered in the locality. The path climbs steeply up the hillside away from Clay House and after a brief spell on the

level, passing rows of terraced houses, climbs even more sharply to provide panoramic views across the valley. Having turned its back on Greetland and Elland now, the way concentrates on glimpses of Halifax and the Wainhouse Tower over on the horizon as it passes between fields and dark drystone walls.

On the right, there are good views of Elland power station, though this hardly enhances the landscape. Just beyond the power lines, the way reaches the edge of North Dean Wood and here there are superb views across the Calder Valley, with Halifax and the Wainhouse Tower tending to dominate the distant skyline. Below you, straddling the valley floor, is the Salterhebble Canal Basin and on the opposite hillside, the outline of Dudwell Church.

The scene below you is an intriguing composite picture typical of this area: the railway viaduct, the factories and open spaces, and the town suburbs with rows of houses creeping up

Clay House, West Vale. This solid old building marks the start of the Calderdale Way. It also contains the Visitors' Centre, giving a fascinating insight into the history and background of Calderdale.

Even at a distance, Wainhouse Tower can be identified as a distinctive landmark, standing out proudly on the horizon for miles around. This octagonal stone folly was built in the early 1870s by J. E. Wainhouse as a dyeworks chimney, which in fact was never used. Containing a spiral staircase of 403 steps and open to the public at certain times, Wainhouse is known locally by another name – the Tower of Spite. Apparently two neighbouring nineteenth-century landowners fell out and as a result, one wilfully built a high wall to maintain and protect his privacy. Not to be outdone, and in a fit of pique, his warring neighbour fired the next shot by constructing the 253-feet high (77-m) tower so that he could see over the wall and across the other man's land. The tale may have become a little exaggerated over the years, but the idea of two grown men going to such extravagant and elaborate lengths to continue their petty squabbling and keep their pride is still quite amusing.

the hillside – they are all there, cluttering the banks of the Calder. Clearly visible as you head west along the path is the village of Copley, beside the viaduct. Copley was built by Colonel Edward Akroyd in the middle of the nineteenth century. Colonel Akroyd, like a number of mill owners, recognized that the conditions under which his employees lived and worked were hard and often appalling. Copley was established, before Saltaire or Acroyden, as part of the move to erect brighter, cleaner premises in purpose-built model villages where workers could live better, healthier lives. However, today the mill has gone and part of Copley is now occupied by sheltered housing.

The route of the path continues west through North Dean Wood, along the side of the valley for some distance, providing continuous, uninterrupted views over to the right. Eventually the path joins the road for a brief spell at Clough Moor Bridge and then strides out to Norland Moor, a windy, gritstone plateau covered in heather. It was bought by public subscription in 1932. Overlooking the Calder and Ryburn valleys, Norland Moor is crisscrossed by a network of footpaths offering plenty of bracing walks and the chance for people to feel the Yorkshire wind in their faces. The reasoning behind its acquisition is explained on the information board at Clay House, West Vale: 'fresh air and recreation'. For the pedestrian outdoor enthusiast, this is unquestionably reason enough.

Soon the path begins to turn away from the buildings of

Halifax and the town of Sowerby Bridge, nestling in the valley below, and heads south down to the road beyond Ladstone Rock. From the trig. point on the westerly edge of the moor, there are views across spectacular Pennine landscapes on the opposite side of the Ryburn Valley.

Join the road and drop down to the New Rock Inn – an isolated position for a pub but welcome none the less. The Calderdale Way turns right here and follows several farm tracks running between drystone walls, eventually joining the road above Ripponden. The descent into the village is a steep

The quaint packhorse bridge at Ripponden. The cobbled bridge over the Ryburn is the focal point of this delightful village. Steep streets lead down to it and at every corner there are glimpses of the narrow valley in which Ripponden lies.

one, though it affords glorious views over this peaceful valley. At the bottom is the picturesque Pennine Farm Museum, open during the spring, summer and early autumn months. It illustrates the living and working environments of a farming family around the middle of the last century.

The museum is near the church of St Bartholomew, situated in the centre of Ripponden. It was founded in 1464 and is within a stone's throw of quaint buildings, twisting alleyways and old stone weavers' cottages clustered around a picturesque pack-horse bridge below the main A58 road. In fact, most of Ripponden's main streets look down on to the bridge and the River Ryburn flowing prettily beneath it. A conservation village, Ripponden was at one time chiefly associated with weaving.

Passing the Conservative Club, the path climbs out of the village to cross several fields, with the road running parallel along the valley floor far below. Descending quite steeply again into the small but delightful village of Mill Bank, the way passes rows of quaint houses and cottages at the bottom of the valley. Like so many villages and towns along the route, the buildings are of familiar Pennine stone – in some ways austere, but so much a part of the backdrop of the hills.

Before the stream, the route turns sharp left and winds through woodland before emerging on to high ground. Here there are glimpses of Halifax and the Wainhouse Tower again – the town and its splendid landmark seemingly never far away. Now the way begins to head for harsh, unpopulated landscapes, so typical of the Pennines. Despite the occasional intrusion of the twentieth century, there is still a sense of timelessness up in these hills and of things unchanged.

Beyond the now defunct Flints Reservoir, as the way begins to turn right, continue for a few steps and you will be treated to a panoramic view roughly incorporating the route of the path ahead of you. It is at this point that hikers on the Calderdale Way first glimpse Stoodley Pike Monument, standing alone on a distant sweep of moorland. Nearer at hand are the buildings of Cragg Vale. This area is populated by sheep, which seem to venture forward quite suddenly from nowhere. Quite gradually at first the path begins to drop down towards Cragg Vale, cutting along tracks and ancient packhorse routes as it does so.

Interestingly, the Poet Laureate Ted Hughes was born at nearby Mytholmroyd and the stark beauty of this landscape provided much of the inspiration for his work. His verses convey vividly the greyness and isolation of these hills when he tells the reader to: 'walk the ridges of ruined stone' and writes that the moors 'hide their edges, showing their possessions only upward to the sky, preferring to be left alone'. The steep descent into Cragg Vale is never less than spectacular.

Passers-by on the route making the climb to Crow Hill often look tired and breathless, and with some justification. It is a sharp pull up for those making the trip. The route of the Calderdale Way spares hikers the arduous climb, instead treating them to glorious views of Cragg Vale, an unspoilt village straddling the floor of this lovely, steeply wooded valley.

Stoodley Pike on the horizon. The dark obelisk is suited to its dramatic surroundings, high in the Pennines.

Cragg Vale to Heptonstall
16 miles (26 km)

Cragg Vale is very much in the heart of textile country. During the last century the Hinchcliffe family owned a number of mills situated along the Cragg Brook, and apart from these mills, little has changed along this peaceful waterway since those days. A century before this development took place, Cragg Vale flourished for a different reason: counterfeit coining took place here until those responsible were caught, tried and later hanged at York.

In the village centre, the route follows the main road briefly and then slips downhill again to arrive at the church of St John the Baptist in the Wilderness. Built in 1839, the church dominates this picturesque wooded setting with a brook chattering noisily nearby. Just beyond the church is The Hinchcliffe Arms, named after the textile family.

The road in front of the inn takes the route of the way up towards Withens Clough and Withens Reservoir on the other side of the valley. It is a winding climb but soon the path reaches level ground, and follows a stony track along the northern edge of the reservoir. Here the way is enclosed by bleak, featureless hills of rough pasture circling the reservoir, divided as always by drystone walls. The fine summer weather gives this stretch a cheerful, acceptable face, but on dark winter days, the landscape can look particularly grim, the hills assuming a raw, inhospitable edge.

The association with the reservoir is a brief one and soon the route is away up into the hills, amid boggy, lumpy pasture, haphazard stone walls and sheep. The only sounds to intrude here are of birds wheeling overhead and the stiff Pennine breezes, bringing with them the scent of sweet, cool air and somehow a rejuvenating sense of well-being.

At Withens Gate you pass the Te Deum Stone, which bears the recognizable inscription 'Te Deum Laudamus' – We Praise Thee, O Lord. Where the stone lies is sacred ground, for when this path was a packhorse route between Cragg Vale and Mankinholes, coffins which were carried this way were ceremoniously lowered here for rest during the journey.

The Te Deum Stone near Stoodley Pike.

NICOLA WASTIE

Returning to the Calderdale Way, the path becomes paved as it crosses the well-signposted route of the Pennine Way, often busy with keen, dedicated walkers as well as casual sightseers up from the villages of Lumbutts and Mankinholes just below. Beneath the point where the routes meet, the Calderdale Way zigzags down the hillside by means of the paved causeway. As you descend the path, you cannot fail to spot the Stoodley Pike Monument again on the nearby moorland summit. The monument was built in 1814 to commemorate the surrender of Paris following the Napoleonic Wars. However, severe Pennine winters weakened its structure and it collapsed in 1854. Happily, it was rebuilt two years later and now stands tall and proud in a commanding position overlooking the hills.

Lumbutts and Mankinholes sit as compatible neighbours in the valley below the monument and now form part of a conservation area. The Water Wheel Tower at Lumbutts has a fascinating industrial background: it once contained three water wheels, one on top of the other, supplied by water siphoned from several dams.

The route follows the road out of Lumbutts and then goes across field paths and farm tracks before you begin the gradual descent into Todmorden, the spire of the Unitarian church clearly visible ahead. The approach to the town is over winding, descending streets of picturesque houses and cottages, conveniently tucked away from the noise and bustle of the main square.

The palatial exterior of Todmorden town hall. The glittering centrepiece of Todmorden once defined the county boundary between Lancashire and Yorkshire.

Todmorden is situated where three valleys converge. At one time it was part of both Lancashire and Yorkshire, with the boundary going through the town hall, a fine, solid building with a most striking façade. Town halls, it seems, are a proud feature in these parts.

The achievements of the Fielden textile family are remembered in Todmorden. It was they who built the town hall, but more importantly, in the eighteenth and nineteenth centuries they established a most successful cotton-spinning industry in the town and, always mindful of the welfare of others, provided work for a large number of people. One member of the family, John Fielden, became an MP and did much to try and help improve the working conditions of factory employees. Todmorden was later dubbed 'Honest John's Town' because of his tireless efforts and upstanding character.

The way leaves this little Pennine town with its bustling centre, open-air market and sturdy old buildings by crossing the canal and then the railway. Up on the slopes again, there are good views over the town and along the narrow valley before you pass Dobroyd Castle, at one time the family home of the Fieldens and now a school. The walk across the tops is a bracing one, with fine Pennine views, and the descent towards Centre Vale provides frequent glimpses of the northern outskirts of Todmorden. Below Buckley Wood, Centre Vale is a park of 75 acres (185 ha) acquired in 1910 by the town council. The Fielden family lived here at one time.

The path returns briefly to the town before climbing steadily back into the hills. It levels out eventually to follow an old packhorse route for a while. In wet weather, this is a bleak landscape of wild, misty moorland and frequent clusters of rocky outcrops. At such times, this eerie, forlorn and forgotten part of the world looks as if it has hardly changed since before the coming of man.

The path crosses Whirlaw Common, keeping to the causeway before following a series of paths and tracks, enjoying a fleeting association with place names that are quaint and bizarre – Wickenberry Clough, East Hey Head, Higher Birks and Great Rock among them. This last landmark is better known locally by another name, Devil's Rock, and here again there are splendid views over the valley. Like so many of these outcrops, the great millstone sculpture seems to rear up out of the landscape like some grotesque prehistoric creature – a confused act of nature, the rocks thrown haphazardly together in a solid, concentrated mass and yet, at first glance, looking fragile enough to topple over at any moment.

Now the way heads out over Staups Moor to Hippins Bridge, and the remote hamlet of Blackshaw Head beyond. The path crosses open farmland before meeting up once again with the Pennine Way as it heads north towards the wild

moorland that helped build its reputation as Britain's toughest and most gruelling long-distance footpath. On more gentle Pennine slopes, the Calderdale Way reaches Heptonstall, a charming olde-worlde village on a ridge between two valleys. It began life as a handloom-weaving community with quaint stone cottages and delightful crooked streets, and today qualifies as a conservation area. Originally, the handloom weavers worked in their homes, but with the coming of steam and the onset of the Industrial Revolution, mills were soon established in the narrow valley below, drawing their power from the swift Pennine streams. A steep road drops down from the village into Hebden Bridge, Heptonstall's close neighbour.

Heptonstall. A village of stone weavers' cottages on a moorland ridge. The sad remains of the fifteenth-century church stand alongside a newer place of worship. The old grammar school houses a museum illustrating life in Heptonstall through the centuries.

Heptonstall to Holdsworth
11 miles (18 km)

Now in the care of the National Trust, Hardcastle Crags lie close to the route of the Calderdale Way and it is worth deviating from the path for a visit. Comprising several steep valleys of broad-leaved woodland and rocky outcrops, Hardcastle Crags is a popular beauty spot, loved by locals as well as by people from further afield. Wild flowers grow here and the woodland is a delightful nature reserve, inhabited by red squirrels, among other creatures.

The climb up towards Pecket Well is steep in places but the final leg, leading to a seat and stile near the Pecket War Memorial, is rewarding, with distant views over Heptonstall and across to Stoodley Pike.

The next stage of the route is along high-level tracks and bridleways as it begins to skirt the edge of Wadsworth Moor. The way runs above a golf course on the right and the disused Cock Hill Quarries on the left. It then crosses Midgley Moor to a distinctive stone obelisk known quaintly as Churn Milk Joan. Believed to be a medieval cross or possibly a boundary stone, the obelisk has a history firmly entrenched in mythology. Local legend claims that a milkmaid died here after finding herself lost on the moors. In poor visibility, it is advisable to leave the moor top and follow the valley floor on the road to Midgley or Jerusalem Farm.

Across Crow Hill, Luddenden Dean, a wooded glen, is a popular haunt for many people. This is hardly surprising, for there are some delightful wooded walks to discover here, making for some a pleasant alternative to the unrelieved expanses of Calderdale's moorland scenery.

The way makes now for the hamlet of Saltonstall, where Richard Saltonstall, a sixteenth-century Lord Mayor of London was born, and then briefly cuts across the south-eastern edge of Warley Moor. The viewpoint on the road beyond the moor provides a good excuse for stopping to rest. From here the path is a grass track up towards Hunter Hill, which at over 1,200 feet (364 m) is one of the highest points on the Calderdale Way.

A stone's throw from the hill are Upper and Lower Brockholes, where there are buses and an inn. Beyond the A629 the way follows pleasant, gentle farm tracks and field paths to the north of Illingworth, a sprawling suburb on the edge of Halifax. There are a number of stiles along this stretch and the landscape gradually takes on a more gentle, pastoral appearance without the harsh, bleak severity of open Pennine moorland.

Holdsworth lies next door to Illingworth. There are four schools sitting in a row here and a number of interesting and distinctive old buildings to see, including Holdsworth House Farm.

Holdsworth to West Vale
14 miles (22 km)

The soft hillsides of the Shibden Valley were worked for iron and coal at one time. Now the scene is a pleasant rural landscape, dotted with fields and trees. Between the villages of

Shelf and Northowram, on a busy street corner, lies the locally famous Stone Chair. Built as a seat for waiting stagecoach passengers in 1737, it looks oddly out of place in today's bustling world.

The way continues to the village of Norwood Green, a pleasant place on the outskirts of Halifax. Passing the White Bear Inn along the main street, notice the pub sign: the name 'White Bear' comes from a ship that was part of the fleet which fought the Armada in 1588.

Beyond the village is Wyke Viaduct, which between 1881 and 1948 carried the Bradford–Huddersfield railway line above its arches. As with the other viaducts on the Calderdale Way, it is a splendid sight, as well as a lasting reminder of the golden age of railway travel. After the village of Bailiff Bridge, with its carpet mills and the Punchbowl Hotel, the walk climbs on to higher ground and soon there are excellent views of Brighouse as you begin the descent towards the town. Apart from the maze of rooftops overlooked by warehouses and factory chimneys, the other most prominent landmarks here are probably the imposing parish church of St Martin's on the near hillside and towards the skyline the huge towers of Elland power station.

Wyke Viaduct near Norwood Green. Viaducts often evoke nostalgic memories of the great railway days of steam and this one, discontinued after the Second World War, is no exception.

Brighouse Canal Basin – now much favoured by boat people in pursuit of leisure. There was a time when this stretch of water enjoyed great commercial success. During the eighteenth century Brighouse was an important canal port following the opening of the Calder and Hebble Canal.

On arriving in Brighouse itself, it is worth pausing to look around this quiet little town. It is the home of both valve and carpet manufacture and general engineering, among other industries, and was an important communications centre in the eighteenth and nineteenth centuries, with good road, rail and canal links. Today Brighouse is best known nationally as a centre for brass band music.

The way heads for Brighouse Canal Basin, built during the 1760s and now crowded with sleek motor cruisers and colourful narrowboats. Leaving Brighouse, the path follows the canal through a semi-industrial landscape and then out into the country again. Beyond Southowram village there are splendid views and a brief return to the Calder before the way returns to the Visitors' Centre at Clay House, West Vale, where the walk ends.

BIBLIOGRAPHY
The Calderdale Way, written and devised by the Calderdale Way Association, is a guide to the circular route, with suggestions for shorter walks using link paths and local transport. It includes maps and sketches, and is available from:
Tourist Information Centre
Piece Hall
Halifax
West Yorkshire HX1 1RS

9 Glyndwr's Way

The fifteenth-century warrior statesman Owain Glyndwr was the great Welsh hero. He was a larger-than-life character in the mould of Dylan Thomas or Richard Burton, and his patriotic fervour would undoubtedly have won approval from today's generation of Welsh nationalists. Born around the middle of the fourteenth century, Glyndwr desperately wanted to establish Wales as an independent nation. His struggle to this end led to rebellion and countless bloody battles. Ultimately, he failed, but the landscape over which this route passes was the very heart of his battleground.

Glyndwr aside, the area abounds with fascinating myths and legends. Although too numerous to chronicle here, they give a colourful, romantic background to the walk. Equally appealing is the scenery, a striking combination of soft hills, fertile valleys and remote, rugged wastelands that will surely bring a glow of excitement to the dedicated long-distance walker.

This is sheep-farming country, isolated, unknown and somewhat inaccessible to the visitor, yet characterizing the true spirit of mid-Wales. There are few obvious signs of commercialism here. Devised by the Planning Department of Powys County Council, Glyndwr's Way is inclined to head for the hills at the earliest opportunity and in places the path is quite tough and unpredictable. The weather, too, is fickle and unpleasantly deceptive in this region. One minute the sun will be shining in a clear, blue sky and the next, the hills and mountains are shrouded in mist and rain. It is vital for those wishing to explore on foot to be prepared for such conditions. In wet and misty conditions it is advisable to avoid the hilltops and keep to the valley alternatives instead.

Beginning in the frontier town of Knighton, renowned for its associations with Offa's Dyke, in hardly any time at all you are climbing high into border country and heading west towards the ruins of Abbey Cwmhir. The next main objective is the little town of Llanidloes and just beyond it Clywedog

Length 120 miles (192 km)
Start Knighton
Finish Welshpool
Going Demanding in some places
Ordnance Survey Maps 125, 126, 135, 136, 148
Waymarking Standard waymarks and Glyndwr's Way signposts in both English and Welsh; a compass and the Ordnance Survey maps covering the route are essential as sections of the path are indistinct

Owain Glyndwr, the Welsh hero
– a significant figure in the
country's history.

Dam, enclosed by spectacular sweeps of hill and open moorland. West of the reservoir the path marches across the Plynlimon foothills, where the landscape is often wild and threatening and the views are some of the best of the entire walk.

The market town of Machynlleth is roughly the half-way mark and there are a number of attractions here, including the site where Owain Glyndwr held parliament and was crowned Prince of Wales. From here the way turns east away from the coast and on through several villages, including Cemmaes Road and Llanbrynmair, before reaching the wooded shores of Lake Vyrnwy.

The last stage is through pleasant rolling countryside as far as Welshpool, where there is much to distract the visitor. The town's major attraction has to be Powis Castle, poised enchantingly on a rock outside the town. Glyndwr's Way continues for a short distance to the village of Hope and finishes at Offa's Dyke.

Accommodation is fairly easy to find along the route and Knighton and Welshpool at the start and finish of the walk are served by buses and trains.

Knighton to Llanbadarn Fynydd
21 miles (34 km)

The walk begins at the heart of Knighton, a pleasant little market town on the River Teme. Knighton's Welsh name is Tref-y-Clawdd, 'The Town on the Dyke' – a reference to nearby Offa's Dyke, 30 feet (9 m) high here with a trench 15 feet (4.5 m) deep beside it. The Dyke is about 1,200 years old and was built by Offa, King of Mercia, in an attempt to defend his kingdom against the Welsh. Nowadays Offa's Dyke lends its name to a long-distance path opened by Sir John Hunt in 1971 and running the length of the frontier from Chepstow in the south to the seaside town of Prestatyn on the north Wales coast.

Knighton is surrounded by wooded hills. The town nestles

An interesting myth suggests that Gwynhwyfar or Guinevere married Arthur at a castle at Knucklas. According to the story, Guinevere's brothers were captured by the giants of Bron Wrgan – a place nearby – but Arthur came to the rescue and slew them. As a result Guinevere's father offered his daughter's hand in marriage to Arthur as a token of appreciation for what he had done.

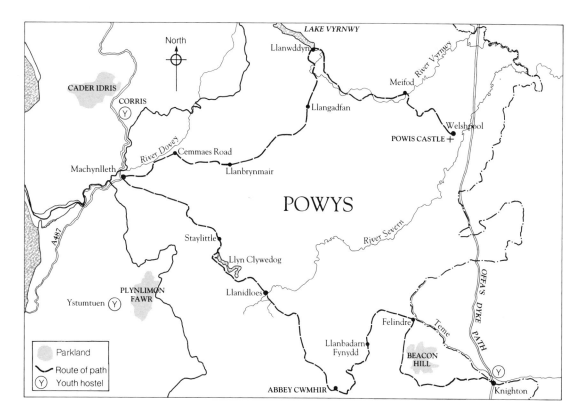

beneath them, its streets steep, its buildings picturesque. At its centre is the distinctive fairytale clock-tower peeping between the rooftops, given to Knighton by Thomas Moore in 1872. This marks the start of Glyndwr's Way and from here the route immediately makes for the outskirts of the town. Where the A488 begins to climb up through the hills, turn right by the foxhound kennels on to a waymarked path.

The approach to Fountain Head is more than impressive. This is a breezy place with wide, unbroken views over the rolling Welsh landscape. Keeping to a ridge, there are glimpses down the valley towards Knucklas.

Beyond Fountain Head the way follows a track heading towards Llancoch. At length it arrives in the little village and at this point the path crosses the tunnel of the Central Wales railway line, which runs between Shrewsbury and Swansea. Now it swings west again, climbing to more than 1,500 feet (454 m) over stretches of exposed moorland. This is wild, untamed country that demands much of the hiker, so be especially careful. The path crosses over Short Ditch, a heather-clad rampart constructed by the English in order to defend Knighton when the town was seen as a possible target for attack by Glyndwr's forces.

The clock-tower at Knighton. Not only does Knighton mark the beginning of the Glyndwr's Way but this charming little town is an ideal base for hill walking in the lovely Welsh Marches. Offa's Dyke is close by.

The route passes the remains of Beacon Lodge, an old house remotely situated miles from any form of civilization. Near the Lodge there are glimpses of Radnor Forest away to the south and beyond this vast landscape of trees and wild, rolling moorland the distant peaks of the Black Mountains are just visible – weather permitting.

Up on Beacon Hill the heather is a bright, dazzling purple and the bracken green and gold. The ground is a deep carpet of rich colours, the scenery some of the finest on this stretch of the walk. Look out for various kinds of flowers here, too, including the cross-leaved heath and the creeping tormentil. Beacon Hill, as its name suggests, is where fires were lit over the years to signify major events or news of national importance. The path skirts round Beacon Hill and then goes northwards to cross Black Mountain.

Past Cefn Pawl there are splendid views across the Teme River Valley to the Kerry Hills beyond. Felindre lies on the banks of the Teme and has several notable features to

distinguish it from other villages in the area. There is a working forge here and an international tug-of-war team whose trophies can be seen in The Wharf Inn, where at this stage of the proceedings you may wish to pause for rest and refreshment.

The next stretch is gentle walking across country, again with pleasant views over the Teme Valley. There are a number of Bronze Age tumuli in this area. Near Felindre is a spot known as Crug-y-Byddar, signified by two raised mounds on opposite banks of the Teme. The larger mound is believed to have been where Uthyr Pendragon, the father of King Arthur, resided. The word 'dragon' was often used metaphorically in early Welsh poetry to suggest warrior or man of strength, and perhaps this is why the dragon is used as the symbol of Wales.

The village of Llanbadarn Fynydd is set on the busy A483 road, but as if to compensate for this, the River Ithon flows prettily past a variety of houses and cottages. The village's name means 'The Church of St Padarn among the Hills'. Padarn, a sixth-century saint, was a disciple of St David,

Bailey Hill – on the approach to Fountain Head. From here 1,200 feet (364 m) above sea level, the views stretch for miles over a landscape of rolling hills and woodland. Down below in the foreground is the outline of Knucklas Viaduct. Knucklas is from the Welsh 'cnwc las', meaning 'green mound'.

patron saint of Wales. The church was rebuilt towards the end of the nineteenth century.

Accommodation is available at Llanbadarn Fynydd, making it the ideal choice for an overnight stop.

Llanbadarn Fynydd to Llanidloes
22 miles (35 km)

From the village the path heads west and then south, making for the ridge of a hill known as Moel-Dod. Here there are views of the Ithon Valley away to the east and a little to the west of the path are the remains of a long-abandoned settlement, New Well. This was a prosperous place around the turn of the century, with facilities that included a shop and a school. Sadly, New Well, like many similar villages, has all but disappeared over the years, as people moved away to find employment in other areas.

Soon the route joins a road running alongside Bachell Brook and you are now in a totally unspoilt, wooded valley. The splendid Manor House on the right as you approach Abbey Cwmhir is mock-Elizabethan style and was built in 1883. Some of the stones used to build it were taken from the old abbey ruins. The setting for Abbey Cwmhir is unusual to say the least. It is a tiny village buried down a quiet lane, a sleepy place seemingly miles from anywhere, surrounded by high hills and slopes thick with forestry plantations.

There is an inn, The Happy Union, which does bed and breakfast and in addition to that there are several houses and a shop. But that is all. It is really the kind of place you would stumble upon only by accident, for it is completely smothered by trees and hills. Quite simply it is hidden, its existence unknown to all but a few. The village takes its name from a large Cistercian abbey, founded in 1143, which was subsequently destroyed by Owain Glyndwr at the beginning of the fifteenth century. Abbey Cwmhir means the 'Abbey of the Long Valley' and it was not uncommon for such monasteries to be built in isolated places like this, with access extremely difficult. Had it been finished, the abbey would have been one of the most impressive in Britain, certainly one of the largest. However, Glyndwr discovered that many of the monks here were English and became convinced they were spies acting under instructions from Henry IV. As a result, its future was immediately doomed.

The present church at Abbey Cwmhir was built during the reign of Queen Victoria, but the style is twelfth-century Gothic. Note The Happy Union Inn opposite, with its curious sign: a man wearing a hat with a leek in it, riding a goat and clasping an ale jug and plate.

Opposite the inn take the track to Clywedog Brook. Beyond

it the path links up with an ancient trackway known as the Monks' Way. Various sources suggest that the Monks' Way was once the main connecting route between Abbey Cwmhir and another monastery at Strata Florida, a few miles away to the west. The trackway eventually arrives in Bwlch-y-Sarnau, emerging in the centre of this remote, windswept village near the Baptist church. You cannot continue the walk without pausing to rest for a while and to admire the delightful northerly views beyond the churchyard. Now the surroundings are a mixture of forest and open moorland, interspersed with rocky outcrops and bleak, windswept ridges. About 2 miles (3 km) west of here is the village of St Harmon, where the famous diarist the Reverend Francis Kilvert lived and worked during the late 1870s.

The way begins this stretch by skirting the slopes of Baily Hill and then turns west to wind erratically through belts of forest. Blaentrinant is in high moorland country, with breathtaking views all around from a height of about 1,300 feet (394 m). Cader Idris rises to almost 3,000 feet (909 m), and the Plynlimon Hills can be seen from here too.

The next views from above the tiny settlement of Newchapel are again magnificent as you look down toward the Severn

The Church at Abbey Cwmhir is nineteenth-century in date but is clearly Gothic in style. Abbey Cwmhir means 'Abbey of the Long Valley' and its romantic, densely wooded setting is delightful. The original church was built with stones from the ruined abbey nearby.

Valley, 500 feet (152 m) below. Newchapel was built in 1740 by the Baptists in association with the Independent Non-conformists.

A little further on is Llanidloes, an attractive old town packed with picturesque buildings, a few hotels and several guesthouses. The early-seventeenth-century timber-framed market hall is Llanidloes's focal point, however, standing on a busy crossroads in the town centre. The old building has a most interesting and distinguished history. Formerly an assize court and the town's lock-up, it was also the setting for some of John Wesley's sermons. In its time, among other roles, it has been used as a Quaker Meeting House, a public library, a wool market and a working men's institute. Today the upper floor is a museum displaying relics from some of the old local lead mines that were once prominent in the area. Below the museum is a cobbled marketplace and gracing the roof of the building is a cupola which contains the market bell, rung on the dot of eight o'clock each evening to signify to shopkeepers and stallholders the end of trading for the day.

Llanidloes to Machynlleth
23 miles (37 km)

Continuing with the walk, the route now heads for the River Severn, where there was once a bridge; reputedly haunted, or so local legend suggests.

Press on along roads until you reach the village of Fan, which 100 years ago witnessed frantic activity of an industrial nature. During the second half of the nineteenth century Fan mine employed over 700 men, producing thousands of tons of lead and zinc ore. Today there is little evidence left of that great mining boom, only a few spoil heaps and the crumbling remains of the old mine buildings.

Close by is Fan Pool, once a reservoir for the mine but now a haven for waterfowl – among the species, a great crested grebe.

The legend of the bridge concerns a Lady Jeffreys. Regarded locally as a miscreant, she was transformed into a water spirit, hovering over the bridge for much of the time. She would watch the ivy grow on the bridge, desperate to see what happened, for only if the ivy covered the keystone in great profusion could her spirit rest in peace. But the ivy was sometimes cut back and Lady Jeffreys' ghost was often seen anxiously pacing up and down until the bridge was destroyed in 1848.

Quickly the path climbs to a track leading to a farm and before long there is a rewarding view of the huge Clywedog reservoir, a magnificent sight as you stumble across it, its curvaceous, man-made boundaries stretching away into the distance. Even more spectacular is the sight of the 212-feet-high (64-m) wall of the dam at the south-eastern end of the reservoir, especially when it is overflowing. Finished in December 1967, Clywedog is 6½ miles (10.4 km) in length and contains something like 11,000 million gallons of water. Its main purpose is to control the flow of the River Severn and to guarantee supplies to the Severn Valley, even in the event of a drought.

The way now heads for the little road that hugs the shore, leading you eventually to the conifer plantation of Hafren Forest – an old Welsh name for the River Severn, which rises 3 miles (4.5 km) to the west. The forest abounds with wild life. On a gloomy day in the middle of winter Clywedog can convey a dark, brooding atmosphere. However, its bleak, isolated setting at the eastern edge of the Plynlimon Hills is quickly

Llyn Clywedog (Clywedog Lake). In creating this reservoir particular care was taken to protect the natural beauty of the area – the green hills and open moorland surrounding it. There are lakeside paths and waymarked nature trails, too, for the enjoyment of the many visitors.

transformed in the summer months into a picnickers' paradise, when tourists and cars sit cheek by jowl on the shoreline. Owain Glyndwr fought a fierce and bloody battle 3 miles (4.5 km) west of here. The assault was surprisingly successful, for in spite of the strength of the opposing army, Glyndwr's men managed to inflict many casualties.

At the northern tip of Llyn Clywedog is the village of Staylittle. Its rather whimsical name may well tickle your curiosity. Legend has it that a local blacksmith reshod horses with such lightning swiftness that his callers were quickly on their way again. Staylittle is well placed for an overnight stop and can provide bed and breakfast accommodation. Above the village centre is the Quaker cemetery, known as the Quaker Garden. According to parish records, it seems Quakers abounded in the area around the beginning of the eighteenth century.

The way passes Rhiw-Defeitty-Fawr Farm before it ascends towards high moorland. From here there are views of the Afon Clywedog and, in the distance to the west, the distinctive summits of the Plynlimon range rising out of a landscape carpeted with forest. The highest summit is 2,468 feet (748 m).

Along this stretch the path follows an old Roman road, which was then a drovers' road and the main stagecoach route between Llanidloes and Machynlleth. Traces of wheel ruts can still be seen here carved into the surface of the centuries-old rock. Follow the path over the summit of Penycrocbren Hill, the site of an old Roman settlement. Below the hill is Dylife, where there is a long-abandoned old metal mine. Dylife – meaning 'place of floods' – still boasts several buildings. Happily one of them is an inn; the other is a rectory. Once this was a bustling, prosperous place with a population of over 1,000, but that was in the days when lead, zinc and copper were plentiful and men worked and lived under appalling conditions. By 1920 the mine was exhausted.

From Dylife the way makes for Foel Fadian, skirting this splendid deep gorge as it heads for the next destination, the village of Aberhosan. From the track you can see Glaslyn Lake, or 'Blue Lake', on the far side of Foel Fadian. This particular stretch of Glyndwr's Way is exceedingly wild; the mountainous landscape is lonely and uninhabited and the views are undeniably spectacular.

The route passes within a stone's throw of Aberhosan. If you are expecting to find refreshment here, you are in for a disappointment. Aberhosan – its name means 'mouth of the River Rhosan' – unfortunately has no cosy inn to provide you with sustenance before beginning the next stage of the walk. Instead, however, there is a church worth making a short detour to see. The path climbs on to exposed ground and beyond the village of Forge joins a winding country road

which leads to Machynlleth after a mile or so. Situated just beyond the half-way point of the walk, the town offers many delights to absorb and entertain visitors. In the middle of Machynlleth is the ornate clock-tower, which looks like a rocket emerging from some underground silo in readiness for lift-off. The clock-tower was given by the Marquis of Londonderry in 1873 and replaces a previous market cross.

It is a quaint old town of bright, bustling streets lined by buildings with handsome façades. There are plenty of shops and hotels in the town, but Machynlleth's main point of interest is the Owain Glyndwr Centre in Maengwyn Street. The old stone building has quite a history to it, for it was on this site in 1404 that Owain Glyndwr held his parliament. The following year he was involved in the Tripartite Indenture. This was a plot to overthrow King Henry IV and subsequently

As time goes by. The clock-tower at Machynlleth is an immense, elaborately decorated structure dominating the town centre. It was presented to Machynlleth in 1873 by the Marquis of Londonderry, a local landowner of some renown.

The Parliament House at Machynlleth – Glyndwr's capital. The stone building is where Owain Glyndwr was proclaimed Prince of Wales. Here he held his first Welsh Parliament during his rebellion against the English Crown.

divide England and Wales between Glyndwr and his fellow conspirators, the Earl of Northumberland and Edmund Mortimer. However, despite assistance from Charles VI of France, the plan failed and a Welsh victory was not accomplished.

Every Wednesday outside the Centre, market stalls appear on the pavement and in July 1986 Her Majesty Queen Elizabeth II paid a memorable visit to the town.

Machynlleth to Llangadfan
23 miles (37 km)

The route to Cemmaes Road initially follows the main A489 road – an unfortunate start to the next stage of the walk. The way now turns inland and heads east towards the finish at Welshpool. Just beyond the little village of Penegoes, it leaves the road at last and makes for open, peaceful country, covered underfoot in places by a thick carpet of bracken. The route is through Abercegir, a small village that sprang into being as a direct result of the wool industry.

The way leaves the village and, once clear of the buildings of this small community, follows an old track which at times is vague and somewhat indistinct as it heads for open hill country. At this point there are splendid uninterrupted views over to Cader Idris. At 2,927 feet (887 m) its dark mass dominates the distant skyline. There are also good views from here over the Aran range and the faint outline of Snowdonia's southern mountain peaks is just visible.

Cemmaes Road sits on the banks of the River Dovey at the point where it meets the Tywyn. In fact, the village is situated in an area renowned for its salmon fishing and again there are excellent views here over typical Welsh scenery. A little to the west is an old house, Mathafarn, where Owain Glyndwr stayed and from where he is said to have travelled by secret tunnel to the Parliament House at Machynlleth.

Briefly, the way keeps to the main A470 road as it heads towards Dolgellau. Leaving the road by a bridge over the Tywyn, it follows a track beside the railway. After a mile or so, the route reaches the settlement of Commins Gwalia, and then follows a minor road and a track to skirt a long plateau known as Mynydd y Cemais, from where there is a superb view of the Dyfi Valley and the River Tywyn. Sheep are fattened here prior to being sold. Many different types of birds can sometimes be seen from here, too, incuding curlews, hawks and buzzards.

The way soon rejoins the A470 again and almost at once reaches Llanbrynmair, situated on the Afon Twymyn, a tributary of the Dovey. The village is spectacularly encircled by hills and mountains and there is undoubtedly an air of rustic rural charm about it. During the middle of the last century Samuel Roberts, or S. R. as he was known, was instrumental here in establishing a newspaper to fight against the exploitation of the tenant farmers in the area. Many of these farmers were victims of greedy landlords who continually demanded higher rents from their tenants. The situation was so desperate that Roberts became their self-appointed spokesman.

The next leg of the walk is scenically one of the most dramatic. It is mostly exposed moorland walking as Glyndwr's Way climbs to 1,000 feet (303 m) or more among isolated hills and bursts of forest – a rugged inhospitable landscape where the passing of the centuries has made little impression. At length the way joins a narrow country road running through the valley of the Afon Gam, an enchanting brook that races along beside the road.

Parting company with the road at Dolwen Farm, the way keeps to a track as it climbs high above the road and the adjoining river. Note the remains of an Iron Age hillfort up among the hills. About 300 feet (91 m) long, the fort commands superb views down towards the next objective on the walk, Llangadfan, and its neighbour Llanerfyl.

The way joins a road again beyond the fort and soon arrives in Llangadfan. The village is above all a paradise for fishermen, being close to so many rivers, including the Banwy, which is stocked with grayling and trout. The name of this village comes from St Cadfan, a sixth-century patron saint of warriors. In later times Llangadfan became the final resting place of the eighteenth-century Welsh poet William Jones.

Llangadfan to Dolanog
17 miles (27 km)

Begin this section by taking the A458 road out of the village and following a footpath beside the River Banwy. Turning right on to the B4395, the way crosses farmland before being engulfed by the trees of the Dyfnant Forest. There are countless species here, including red cedar, Scots pine and Douglas fir.

Coming at last upon Lake Vyrnwy is an agreeable experience. It is, after all, one of the scenic joys of Glyndwr's Way, though the surroundings are not nearly as wild and moody as those of Clywedog. Enclosed by high green hills and with gentle wooded slopes lining its shores, the lake has an almost continental flavour about it.

The reservoir, of course, supplies water to Liverpool and other communities along the route, up to 45 milion gallons a day in fact. Owned by the Severn–Trent Water Authority, Vyrnwy was one of Britain's first reservoirs, but in order for work to go ahead it was necessary to resite the village of Llanwddyn, which at that time lay along the floor of the valley. An Act of Parliament in 1880 allowed Liverpool Corporation to begin work on the reservoir and by 1892 the first water from Vyrnwy reached the city of Liverpool. Two plaques signify major achievements in the history of Lake Vyrnwy. One denotes the laying of the first stone in 1881 and the other refers to a tablet unveiled on 16 March 1910 by His Royal Highness The Prince of Wales to celebrate the completion of the works authorized by parliament.

The route leaves Llanwddyn by following the winding B4393 away from the village and up the hillside. On a sharp hairpin bend, it joins a narrow country road with glimpses of the Afon Efyrnwy (River Vyrnwy) drifting through the valley over on the right. The way keeps to minor roads and forest tracks as far as the village of Llwydiarth.

Continuing with the walk, the route now runs south-east of the village immediately beside the Vyrnwy for nearly a mile. Then it swings away from the river, crossing farmland to join the B4382. Opposite the turning to Dolwar Fach, home of Ann

Griffiths, the eighteenth-century composer of Welsh hymns, the way leaves the road and climbs up to Allt Dolanog, on the summit of which is an Iron Age hillfort.

Dolanog to Welshpool
14 miles (22.4 km)

The final section of the walk begins by crossing the stone bridge over the B4382 and then following the south bank of the Vyrnwy. The path keeps to the river bank for some time, the river cutting deep into wooded country now. In a while, the way joins a track running parallel with the river and after a mile or so stumbles upon Pontrobert. The village has a stone bridge built in the seventeenth century.

The way heads east out of Pontrobert, passing the entrance to Dolobran Hall, which has close associations with finance. The Hall was built in the seventeenth century by Charles Lloyd, whose family established the bank of the same name.

Near Dolobran Hall is an old Quaker Meeting House, where in 1662 a meeting attended by Lloyd was broken up and a number of people, including Lloyd, were arrested. In those days the religious practices of Quakers were banned and Lloyd himself was imprisoned in Welshpool jail, where he later died.

Just before reaching Meifod, the path climbs to the top of

Welshpool. With its bustling streets and black-and-white timber-framed buildings, this is a particularly attractive market town in the Severn Valley. The Montgomery Canal provides good recreational facilities.

Gallt yr Ancr, where there are excellent views to the south across the valley of the Vyrnwy. Dropping down from the hill, the way reaches Meifod, a charming village with an inn and overnight accommodation.

The last 10 miles (16 km) or so between Meifod and the town of Welshpool are mainly over forest tracks and quiet country roads. The scenery is pleasant and varied here, with good views and, on occasions, one or two climbs. Near the fortification at Fronlas is a place known as Cobham's Garden.

Some way south of this spot the way runs along the edge of Big Forest. Beyond Pant Wood, it reaches the road at Stonehouse Farm, and from here it is a short walk to Welshpool.

You can take boat trips and hire canoes on the Montgomery Canal, while the centre of this busy market town has many fine Georgian buildings worth seeing, particularly in the vicinity of Broad Street. The Powysland Museum is open most days and includes interesting exhibitions of local history and archaeology.

To the south of the town and within easy walking distance is Powis Castle, owned by the National Trust. Built by Welsh princes around the beginning of the thirteenth century, the castle perches spectacularly on a rock above landscaped gardens designed by Capability Brown in the early nineteenth century. There is much for visitors to see, including elegant terraces,

---

It is only a field now, but Cobham's Garden has an interesting tale to tell concerning Lord Cobham, or Sir John Oldcastle as he was otherwise known, who distinguished himself by serving both Henry IV and V well during the Welsh wars. But Cobham was a strong supporter of a religious reformer known as Wycliffe, whose followers were called Lollards. As a result, Cobham was sent by Henry IV to the Tower of London. He managed to escape in 1413, and immediately went into hiding in Wales. Henry announced there would be a reward of 1,000 marks for anyone apprehending him. Edward de Chereton, who was also under suspicion, at once sought to take advantage of the situation by trying to find Cobham and claim the reward. Once de Chereton had found Cobham, at the place now known as Cobham's Garden, with the assistance of an armed mob he set upon him. Cobham almost managed to escape, but a woman stopped him by breaking his leg with a stool. Cobham was later condemned to death, and died in a most horrible manner, suspended from the gallows while a fire burned beneath him.

The Welshpool and Llanfair Light Railway. 8 miles (13 km) long, established in 1903 to carry local people to market, the railway closed in 1956. However, enthusiasts ensured that the line was eventually reinstated and today the railway is as popular as ever.

Below Romantic Powis Castle. It rises proudly above sumptuous gardens – a horticulturalist's dream. Everywhere you look there are long terraces, shrubs and trees. The imposing castle, built of limestone and granite, has been occupied continuously for more than 500 years.

herbaceous borders and a splendid profusion of trees, plants and shrubs. Officially the walk ends 2 miles (3 km) east of Welshpool at the village of Hope, where Glyndwr's Way joins Offa's Dyke Path.

BIBLIOGRAPHY
A set of sixteen leaflets describing the route in fairly general terms, with maps and illustrations, is available from:
    Powys County Council Planning Department
    Powys County Hall
    Spa Road East
    Llandrindod Wells
    Powys LD1 5LG
For up-to-date information on the route contact:
    Recreation Paths Officer
    Offa's Dyke Centre
    West Street
    Knighton
    Powys LD7 1EW
    Tel. (0547) 528192
It is well worth visiting the Centre before beginning the walk.

10 The Heart of England Way

The Heart of England Way was established for several reasons. First, to provide a route through varied central England scenery, offering an interesting and unusual insight into the rural heart of the Midlands, Shakespeare country and the rolling hills of the North Cotswolds. Second, to link two other long-distance routes – the Staffordshire Way to the north and the Cotswold Way at its start in the south. It is a delightfully green walk, running across peaceful, pastoral landscapes and past historic houses, picturesque inns, hidden churches and scenic stretches of river and canal. Yet surprisingly, in its early and middle stages, the route passes close to the huge urban and industrial sprawl of the West Midlands – though, thankfully, it never really gets within sight of it.

The Heart of England Way was almost thirteen years in the making. It was conceived in 1978 by a group of walking clubs and, in its initial stages of development, was very much a voluntary effort. In time, however, the Countryside Commission and four local authorities added their weight by negotiating with farmers and landowners, and eventually the route's proud pioneers saw the fruits of their labours when, in October 1990, the Heart of England Way was officially opened at Alcester.

The walk begins at the northern tip of Cannock Chase, a wooded playground much loved by locals and tourists alike and designated as an area of outstanding natural beauty. Fallow deer can sometimes be seen amid the trees and across the open spaces. Once this was a royal hunting ground, favoured by kings and noblemen.

Lichfield Cathedral, begun in 1195 and finished 130 years later, is one of the smallest cathedrals in Britain and also one of the loveliest. The city was home of Dr Samuel Johnson, the writer and lexicographer, and the house where he was born is now a museum.

Without doubt, the second half of the walk south of Meriden has greater beauty and a higher degree of historic interest.

Length 80 miles (128 km)
Start Milford near Stafford
Finish Chipping Campden
Going Mostly easy, level walking
Ordnance Survey Maps 127, 128, 139, 140, 150, 151
Waymarking Arrows and coloured discs with 'Heart of England Way' set against a cluster of trees

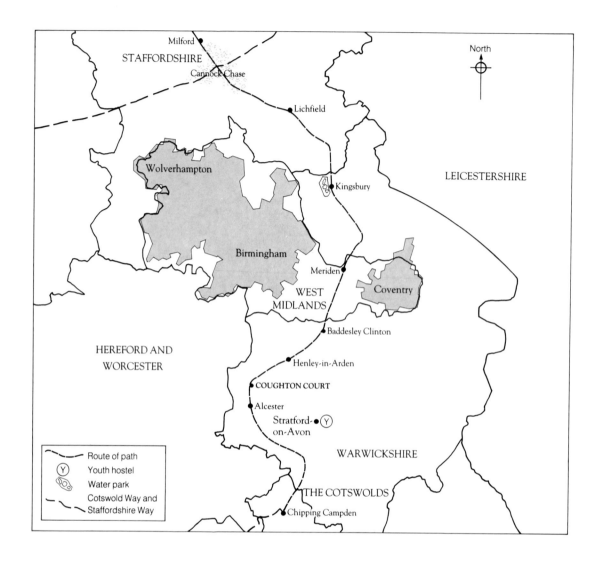

Map legend:

- - - Route of path
(Y) Youth hostel
Water park
Cotswold Way and
Staffordshire Way

Around the enchanting old towns of Henley-in-Arden and Alcester are the remains of the Forest of Arden, which once covered 200 square miles (518 sq km). This was where Shakespeare set *As You Like It*. His spirit is everywhere in this part of the country, in the Warwickshire towns and villages he loved so dearly and in the ancient taverns where he drank so enthusiastically.

Towards the finish, the way passes close to productive market gardens with good views across the lush Vale of Evesham. The last few miles, too, offer suitably dramatic scenery as the route crosses the northern foothills of the Cotswolds to reach Chipping Campden, one of the area's

Opposite Cannock Chase. A favourite haunt of ramblers, who have access to its many tracks, pools and forest rides. Once a dense oak woodland, today it is a mere shadow of its former self.

major tourist attractions and a delightful place in which to finish the Heart of England Way.

Accommodation can be found in most of the towns and villages on the route. Camping sites are limited. There are buses from Stafford to Cannock Chase and at Chipping Campden at the end of the walk. There is also a British Rail mainline station at Stafford and coach services from Birmingham to Stafford and Cannock.

Milford to Lichfield
11½ miles (18 km)

Cannock Chase provides an oasis of much-needed peace and scenic beauty only a few miles from the industrial heartland of the Midlands. Hundreds of years before modern families and the motor car, the Chase was a royal forest where Plantagenet kings hunted game and trees grew in such profusion that you could easily get lost among the huge oaks. Today the trees are fewer but the beauty of the area is no less impressive. Within its 26 square miles (67 sq km) there are picnic sites, information centres, open spaces and pleasant woodland walks to enjoy. Seen from most parts hereabouts is British Telecom's local landmark, a concrete radio transmission tower which is about 1,000 feet (303 m) above sea level. It looks oddly out of place among the trees.

A mile or so from the start of the way are the German and Commonwealth Cemeteries, which are worth a visit. The German military cemetery contains the well-tended graves of all German Armed Forces who died on British soil during the First and Second World Wars, including the first Zeppelin crew shot down over Britain during the First World War.

The Heart of England Way begins at the Tourist Information Office at Milford. Nearby and worth a visit is Shugborough Hall, eighteenth-century home of the Earls of Lichfield. Enlarged and altered between about 1750 and 1806, the house has collections of French and English china, silver, furniture and paintings. Close by is the Staffordshire County Museum, which includes re-creations of nineteenth-century life.

From Milford the way heads south across Cannock Chase to the gnarled remains of Anson's Scots pine trees, planted late in the eighteenth century to celebrate the voyage of Admiral Anson round the world in 1740. The path heads for the Boulderstone, a huge granite relic from the Ice Age, and then briefly follows the Staffordshire Way before taking a woodland walk to Marquis Drive. This is the heart of Cannock Chase, a silent area of beech, pine and silver birch trees and frequent bracken-covered tracts of land.

From the start as far as the fort at Castle Ring the route is mainly over woodland tracks and paths. It crosses the A460

Cannock–Rugeley road about ½ mile (0.8 km) from Smarts Buildings and then heads for the hamlet of Wandon, 1 mile (1.5 km) to the south-east.

Beyond it the path cuts through forestry plantations of Beaudesert Old Park, once the estate of the First Marquis of Anglesey. A steep climb brings you to Castle Ring, an Iron Age hillfort almost 800 feet (242 m) above sea level and the highest point on Cannock Chase. There are good views from here, though the trees tend to restrict the vistas. However, there are tantalizing glimpses of Lichfield Cathedral's famous three spires, known as the 'Ladies of the Vale', from the nearby reservoir. The route to this charming and historic old city is over gentle farmland and along quiet country roads.

Lichfield has much to see apart from the cathedral, but do go there even if only to gaze at the splendour of its west front, a feast of magnificent intricate carving. It boasts 113 statues of figures from the Old Testament, the Holy Family, the Apostles, Saints, Bishops and Kings of England, including Edward the Confessor and William the Conqueror.

The Samuel Johnson Birthplace Museum on the corner of Breadmarket Street is where Johnson was born on 18 September

Ancient Lichfield, where the magnificent soaring spires of the cathedral, known as the 'Ladies of the Vale', overlook the water. Built of red sandstone, it is one of the smallest and most heavily restored cathedrals in the country.

1709, at which time the building was his father's bookshop. The museum contains many interesting relics from his life, including some of his letters and manuscripts, his walking stick and his favourite armchair. Johnson attended Lichfield Grammar School and after his death, in 1784 he was buried in Westminster Abbey. An imposing statue of him overlooks the museum.

Lichfield to Kingsbury
13½ miles (22 km)

The route out of Lichfield is along the A51, heading roughly south-east. Once clear of the main road, you are in open country again, the way following clear tracks and paths to reach the A5 near the village of Weeford. Beyond the A5 the way crosses the Black Brook before traversing rolling hills and farmland. Not far from here is a place known as Hints. Hardly a typically English-sounding name for a village, its origins are thought to be Welsh, where the word '*hynt*' means road. Its close proximity to Watling Street, once an important and strategic Roman road and now the A5, might explain how it got its name.

At Brockhurst Farm the way heads east towards Drayton Bassett. Across the fields to the left as you approach the village is Drayton Manor Park. The house, now demolished, was once the home of Sir Robert Peel, the distinguished prime minister and founder of the British Police Force in 1829. Nowadays the grounds of the house take the form of a pleasure park, which includes a 15-acre (37-ha) zoo, amusements and catering facilities.

The way leaves behind the buildings of Drayton Bassett and joins the Birmingham and Fazeley Canal, following the cut for about 2 miles (3 km) to Kingsbury Water Park. This is a sprawling and picturesque amenity area of a few hundred acres created by Warwickshire County Council from a maze of exhausted sand and gravel pits which now form the setting for a variety of pursuits, including sailing and fishing. There is an information centre here and the chance to see different species of wildlife.

From here the path heads for the parish church of St Peter and St Paul at Kingsbury up on the hill. Before reaching the church it crosses the River Tame at a picturesque reach just below the churchyard. Take a look in the church. The nave is Norman and a past clergyman from here, Henry Cary, a classics scholar who is best remembered for his translation of Dante, is buried in Westminster Abbey beside Samuel Johnson.

Kingsbury to Meriden

13 miles (21 km)

The route is through the centre of Kingsbury and then over the Birmingham–Derby railway line. Away to the left is one of Britain's largest oil-storage depots in a side road on the edge of the village. In sharp contrast, the next thing to catch the eye is a rifle range. Keep to the boundary and be alert when the red flag is flying. Soon the route of the path changes direction and begins to head south, skirting the village of Hurley and on to the unfortunately named Foul End.

Whitacre Heath is a larger village and here there are several inns and a village store. South of the village the path crosses another railway line and then cuts between the line and Shustoke Reservoirs on the right. The two reservoirs, one much smaller than the other, were built in the nineteenth century and now supply water to nearby Nuneaton and Coventry. On the south side of the reservoirs lies the village, with its green and lines of houses and cottages. The church contains the tomb of Sir William Dugdale, the well-known antiquary who was born at the former rectory.

The way heads south again through wooded countryside, a reminder that once this entire area was part of the Forest of Arden. Much has changed since then and most of the forest has long since disappeared. However, the district still provides plenty of pleasant, undulating countryside dotted with woodland and wild flowers, and at times it is hard to believe that the path is only a stone's throw away from the vast urban sprawl of Birmingham and Coventry, even though the pace of twentieth-century life is suddenly brought home with the noisy intrusion of the M6 Motorway several miles south of Shustoke.

Meriden is roughly the half-way point for the Heart of England Way. It has an even greater claim to fame than that, however, for the village is situated at the central point of England – a boast that is marked by the medieval wayside cross on the green.

The memorial at the eastern end of the green remembers those cyclists who gave their lives in the Second World War, and the seat in its stone surround at the opposite end is in memory of a devoted cycling enthusiast who died in September 1956. The seat was erected on behalf of all cyclists by the Cyclists' Touring Club. Meriden is also the venue for archery contests, with the headquarters of the Woodmen of Arden, one of the oldest archery societies in England, nearby.

The green is fringed by shops, houses and pretty cottages and there are opportunities for refreshment as well as overnight accommodation in the village.

Meriden to Henley-in-Arden
16 miles (26 km)

The Heart of England Way heads for the churchyard to start with and then crosses fields to Berkswell. The path cuts through the parkland and past the Norman church of St John the Baptist, which is prettily situated within it. The earliest part of the church dates from about 1150. Note the interesting and unusual gabled and timbered porch.

Before you reach the church note the odd-looking stocks on the village green. According to local legend the five holes were intended to detain a wilful villager with a peg leg as well as his two constant companions. The sixteenth-century Bear Inn, once The Bear and Ragged Staff, has links with Cromwell.

Beyond the church the way skirts the southern edge of Berkswell Park, with its rhododendrons and splendid views of the lake and the Hall on the far side of it. Balsall Common is close by – a sprawling residential village near Coventry. Adjacent Balsall Street is smaller. Close to the path in this district is Temple Balsall, with its thirteenth-century church, St Mary, built by the Knights Templars and restored in 1849 by Gilbert White.

Temple Balsall was a Preceptory of the Knights Templar. After the papal suppression, however, the property passed to the Knights Hospitallers, who were subsequently suppressed by the Act of Dissolution under Henry VIII. Later, Lady Katherine Levison founded a hospital here in 1677, as well as an almshouse for twenty aged and impoverished women. In the nearby cemetery lies Henry Williams, who composed the tune for the famous First World War marching song 'It's a long way to Tipperary'.

After Temple Balsall the route follows paths across pleasant farming country as far as the A41 Birmingham road at Chadwick End. It continues across the fields on the other side of the road, within sight of a Poor Clare's Convent on the left. The way crosses a country lane and then enters the grounds of Baddesley Clinton Hall, a moated late-fifteenth-century manor house now in the ownership of the National Trust. At various times it has been the home of the Clintons and the Bromes, and from 1500 the Ferrers family lived there. A visit is recommended if time permits as there are some interesting features to see, including the walled garden, kitchens, library, Great Hall and Chapel. Baddesley Clinton Hall also has a priest hole, seen from the kitchens, where several persecuted members of the clergy hid during the Reformation.

The walk to the neighbouring church through an avenue of overhanging oak and sycamore trees is a delight. There is almost an air of Jane Austen about it. At the end of the wooded path the parish church lies silent and undisturbed in a forgotten corner. There is a somewhat macabre story to tell about Nicholas Brome, one-time Lord of the Manor at Baddesley Clinton, who is buried in an unusual spot in the churchyard here. Brome was an evil double killer whose second victim was the local vicar. Consumed by feelings of guilt over what he had done, he asked to be buried at the entrance to the church so that worshippers entering it would tread on his grave.

After the grounds of Baddesley Clinton, the way is again over fields through Rowington Green to Rowington. The church of St Lawrence is on a bend in the road at one end of the village. Opposite the church a quiet lane takes the route of the path down to a bridge over the Grand Union Canal. From here it is a short walk to Lowsonford, where there is a bridge over the Stratford-on-Avon Canal and an inn, The Fleur de Lys.

For a while the way follows the route of an old branch railway, which was discontinued during the First World War. Soon the path swings away from the old railway line to run parallel with it as far as Henley-in-Arden.

The ancient Guildhall at Henley-in-Arden.

NICOLA WASTIE

As you approach the village of Beaudesert, Henley's neighbour, the Mount is all that remains of the twelfth-century De Montfort Castle. There are good views from the top of the grass-covered 'motte and bailey' earthworks across typical Arden countryside. Just beyond the remains beside the River Alne is the twelfth-century church of St Nicholas, with its Norman architecture. Nearby is a row of pretty cottages and only 300 feet (90 m) or so from this setting is Henley-in-Arden's mile-long main street, with its quaint oak-timbered buildings and historic attractions.

The half-timbered Guildhall dates from 1448 and is one of the town's real treasures, as is the fifteenth-century parish church of St John the Baptist next door. There are several inns, which give Henley much 'olde-worlde' charm to delight the tourists – among them The White Swan across from the church, which dates from the beginning of the seventeenth century. There are other inns and hotels for overnight accommodation if needed.

Henley-in-Arden to Long Marston
17 miles (27 km)

The route continues in a westerly direction after Henley-in-Arden, making now for Bannams Wood. The woodland has been designated a Site of Special Scientific Interest. Not far away from here it is worth making a small detour to look at the unrestored Warwickshire church of the Holy Trinity at Morton Bagot, located in a peaceful rural setting next door to some ancient farm buildings and surrounded by rolling hills and fields.

Returning to the path for the next mile or so, the route is through soft wooded country as it starts to approach the town of Alcester. Further detours can be made on this stretch. To the east across the fields is the village of Great Alne, where there is a curiously named inn, The Mother Huff Cap Inn. Huff Cap is a colloquialism for the froth or head on a drink. West of the path lies Coughton Court, a mainly Elizabethan house now owned by the National Trust. The house was inherited by the Throckmorton family and in one of the rooms of the great central gatehouse in November 1605 the wives of some of those involved in the Gunpowder conspiracy waited anxiously for news. The house is open to the public.

Approaching the northern outskirts of Alcester now, the route passes close to another National Trust acquisition, the Kinwarton Dovecote. This is a fourteenth-century circular dovehouse with an impressive ogee doorway. The dovecote is open to the public (the key can be obtained next door at Glebe Farm).

Alcester is a lovely old market town lying at the confluence of two rivers, the Arrow and the Alne. It has a number of

Opposite Wild flowers beside the towpath. The way crosses the Grand Union Canal, where it runs through a deep cutting near Rowington. The bustling inland waterway, alive with colourful narrowboats and cruisers, dates back to the beginning of the twentieth century.

Coughton Court can boast a noble gatehouse and many relics of the Throckmorton family, in whose possession the house has been since the early fifteenth century. One member of the family became the secret bride of Sir Walter Raleigh and in 1583 there was the Throckmorton plot against Elizabeth I.

enchanting timber-fronted buildings – particularly those in Butter Street, which is too narrow for cars, and Malt Mill Lane, which has the oldest house in Alcester. The parish church of St Nicholas overlooks the old streets, and adjacent to it is the seventeenth-century town hall.

Ragley Hall, seat of the Marquis of Hertford, lies a mile or so to the south-west of Alcester. It was built by Robert Hooke in 1680 and today is one of the best stately homes in the Midlands.

The way leave Alcester by making for Oversley Green to the south of the town. Beyond the little hamlet there are good views from Primrose Hill across to Alcester and to the route of the path stretching north towards Henley-in-Arden. Oversley Wood, which is within sight of the way, offers a peaceful haven of conifers underplanted with oaks. The wood is in the care of the Forestry Commission.

Next is the church at Wixford, which is almost in a secret place up a long narrow lane. The lane forms part of Ryknild Street, an old Roman road which became the A435 at Alcester and then goes north to Redditch. St Milburgas's is eleventh century in date and the little thatched building in the right-hand corner of the churchyard was reputedly once a stable where the vicar tethered his horse during services. The idea of the clergyman arriving by horse conjures up some charming images.

Bidford-on-Avon. Shakespeare composed a doggerel here after a drinking session. The Avon flows through the pretty village and above the river is the ancient bridge, with its eight irregular arches.

Historic Alcester. Designated a conservation area, Alcester includes many quaint timber-fronted buildings. There is evidence of Roman occupation here and two roads which converge in the town date from that period.

Opposite The weir at Barton. The village has some fine seventeenth century buildings, including the quaint, delightfully named Cottage of Content pub. This is fertile fruit-growing country.

Wixford village is a short distance away. Here there is a pub, The Fish Inn, beside the River Arrow. A sign on the far wall announces that 'William Shakespeare probably drank here' – one of a number of hostelries in the area where the Bard is reputed to have enjoyed a drink or two.

The path continues beside the River Arrow. On this stretch fishermen can often be spotted sitting patiently along the river bank. Near the road the way passes beside a small waterfall and then crosses fields and water meadows to Broom. The village street is long and straight, with Broom Mills at one end and the part-timbered Broom Tavern half-way along it. The way crosses the street and then briefly joins the road at the point where it meets a dismantled railway. Then it is a short walk to the centre of Bidford-on-Avon, a delightful riverside village with a wide fifteenth-century bridge. Its pretty setting is probably best appreciated from the recreation area on the south

Like so many towns and villages in the area, Bidford claims to have Shakespearean associations. Apparently The Old Falcon Inn, no longer a tavern but a distinctive-looking building of Cotswold stone with mullioned windows, was once a favourite watering hole, where Shakespeare composed the following verses after a particularly heavy drinking session:

> Piping Pebworth, dancing Marston,
> Haunted Hillborough, hungry Grafton,
> Dodging Exhall, Papist Wixford,
> Beggarly Broom and drunken Bidford.

It is claimed that Shakespeare and his companions, members of the 'Bidford Society of Sippers', retired to lie under a crabapple tree after their revelry.

bank. Here the scene is a wide, colourful stretch of the Avon, often alive with hectic narrowboat activity and throngs of tourists. The tower of St Lawrence's church can be seen peeping through the trees beyond the bridge.

The way joins forces as far as neighbouring Barton with the Stratford–Marlcliff footpath, which stretches for 9 miles (11.5 km) along the banks of the Avon and is well waymarked with arrows.

Barton is a pretty place with a weir beside the lock and the enchanting Cottage of Content pub and restaurant next door. There are fruit orchards between here and the next village, Dorsington. This is the home of the Domestic Fowl Trust, which has a most interesting collection of domestic fowl and rare breeds from many parts of the world.

Long Marston is notable for several reasons apart from the long main street which provided the inspiration for its name. It is a village associated with Morris dancing and this probably explains the reference to 'dancing Marston' in Shakespeare's verse. Charles II is said to have stayed at King's Lodge during his escape after the Battle of Worcester in 1651. Posing as a servant named Will Jackson, he worked in the kitchens undetected by Roundhead troops and nor did his identity give rise to suspicion among the other servants. The church at Long Marston has a distinctive saddleback tower rising from grey shingles.

Long Marston to Chipping Campden
9 miles (14 km)

The way crosses the A46 about a mile from the village and then makes for Lower and Upper Quinton. As well as a number of

Journey's end at Chipping Campden. With its Cotswold setting, historic buildings and splendid Jacobean market hall, this is a mecca for tourists.

thatched and timber-framed cottages at Lower Quinton, there is The College Arms, which displays the arms of Magdalen College, Oxford. The college owns land in the area.

Upper Quinton, to the south, is smaller. Above it and beside the route of the path lies Meon Hill, 637 feet (193 m) high and crowned by the ramparts of an Iron Age hillfort. The hill top has been the setting for rumoured acts of witchcraft in recent years. The way into Mickleton is between giant greenhouses in the heart of market-gardening country.

Mickleton lies at the northern foot of the Cotswolds, an attractive village with a long and winding street as well as inns and overnight accommodation. The houses are a mixture of thatch, timber and Cotswold stone. Medford House and the parish church should be seen if time permits.

There is a gradual climb through the hills from Mickleton to Kiftsgate Court and, beyond it, the gardens of Hidcote Manor – 289 acres (714 ha) of land owned by the National Trust which include many rare trees and shrubs, as well as rhododendron bushes and camellias.

Now the way begins to explore the unique beauty of the Cotswolds as it makes for Chipping Campden. The tree-lined drive to Mickleton Hills Farm gives teasing glimpses of the rolling landscape before the way crosses the mouth of the Campden railway tunnel on the Oxford–Worcester line.

No visit to the Cotswolds is complete without a look at Chipping Campden and, after the peace of the hills, this is a bustling place in which to finish the Heart of England Way. A prosperous market town and wool-trading centre throughout the Middle Ages, its buildings of mellow stone, medieval doorways and mullioned windows add a final touch of class to this fine Cotswold showpiece. Only the cars and coaches and the constant hordes of sightseers filling the many gift shops and tea rooms seem to threaten its charm. One of the chief attractions is the gabled Jacobean market hall in the high street, owned by the National Trust and built 'for the sale of cheese, butter and poultry'. Another feature is the splendid perpendicular church, built in the traditions of the wool merchants with an elegant fifteenth-century pinnacled tower.

BIBLIOGRAPHY
The Heart of England Way, by John Roberts, contains maps, photographs and sketches, and detailed directions. There are also suggestions about transport and accommodation. It is available from:
Walkways
4 Gilldown Place
Birmingham
West Midlands B15 2LR

11 The Coed Morgannwg Way

The second half of the twentieth century has brought much change to the industrial face of south Wales. The old working pits of the Rhondda have closed and the landscape is no longer blighted by endless coal tips and iron workings. Industry still plays a key role here, but these days the factories are smarter and cleaner and the grimy smoke of the chimneys has long gone.

Surprisingly, at the very heart of industrial south Wales there is some fine walking country – peaceful green valleys and vast expanses of forest, through which runs the Coed Morgannwg Way, a truly delightful walk over ancient Celtic tracks which links three imaginatively designed country parks. It is a solitary route, passing few towns or villages along the way, and in the main it is over Forestry Commission land. Coed Morgannwg, which roughly translated means Forest of Glamorgan, forms the largest area of forest in Wales and species to be found here include oak, spruce, larch, pine and poplar.

The path begins in the Dare Valley Country Park, just outside Aberdare, and the first section, which heads west towards Craig y Llyn, is probably the least wooded stretch of the whole walk. Without doubt, the lonely moorland here makes you feel that you are completely removed from the rest of humanity.

At nearly 2,000 feet (606 m), Craig y Llyn is the highest mountain in Glamorgan and a well-known local landmark and picnic spot at the northern end of the Rhondda valleys. The views from the top are breathtaking and after such an exhilarating experience you could be forgiven for thinking that the rest of the Coed Morgannwg Way is something of an anticlimax, but that is not true. Such is the isolated beauty of this walk that in spite of the ever-present lines of trees, there is seldom a moment in its entire length when the scenery is dull or uninteresting.

After Craig y Llyn the route follows a series of scenic paths

Length 36 miles (58 km)
Start Dare Valley Country Park, near Aberdare
Finish Margam Country Park, near Port Talbot
Going Relatively easy though strenuous in some places
Ordnance Survey Map 170
Waymarking The path is clearly signposted with a series of posts showing a dark-green footprint against a white background

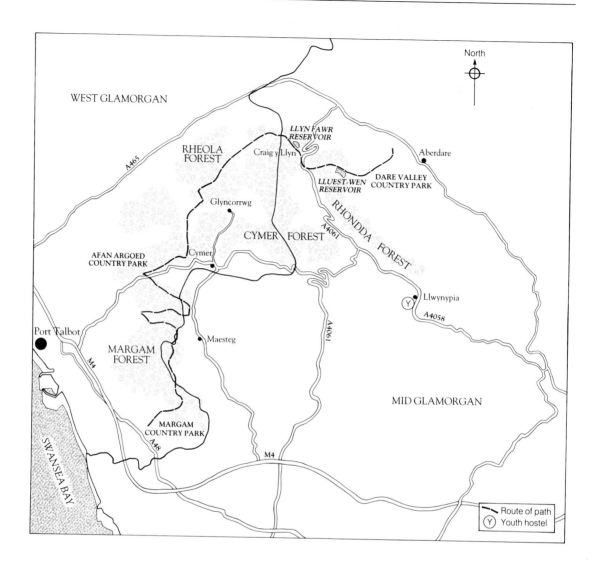

and tracks between the Neath and Afan valleys which leads eventually to Afan Argoed Country Park. This is a little beyond the half-way stage and includes a popular picnic and recreation area for families and walkers.

The second half of the Coed Morgannwg Way is no less spectacular, with a steady climb through the trees to reach Garn Wen, where there are magnificent views. Beyond the village of Bryn, which serves as an unexpected reminder of civilization, the way returns to peaceful woodland scenery before reaching Margam Country Park, outside Port Talbot. The park, which is run by West Glamorgan County Council, is a delightful and interesting spot in which to finish the walk. Daylight permitting, it is possible to complete the route in a day, but to do so would leave little or no time for the various attractions en route.

Accommodation is scarce on the Coed Morgannwg Way though easier to come by in the vicinity of the start and finish. There are bus services at either end of the route.

Dare Valley Country Park to Craig y Llyn
6 miles (10 km)

The Coed Morgannwg Way begins about a mile to the west of Aberdare, a town with a number of striking buildings and several churches of note. The old church of St John is twelfth century in date and has been largely restored. John Ruskin summed up its ancient traditions and lasting qualities when he wrote in his preface to *The History of St John's Church*: 'The greatest story of a building is not in its stones nor its gold but in its age.' In the town centre stands St Elvan's Church, built during the middle of the nineteenth century. Its tall spire seems to make it a focal point of Aberdare as you climb the steep streets leading away from the town.

The Dare Valley Country Park, which was officially opened in 1973, comprises 480 (1,186 ha) acres of land, much of which was once covered by unsightly coal spoil tips. With plenty of hard work and not a little imagination, the head of the valley was reclaimed to provide a delightful amenity area which really offers something for everyone. Many activities are organized by the Ranger Service and there are nature trails to explore, rare species of wildlife to observe and a whole host of other

The start of the Coed Morgannwg Way near the Visitors' Centre in the Dare Valley Country Park.

NICOLA WASTIE

Dare Valley Country Park. The way heads west through the park, which is a naturalist's delight, inhabited by foxes, badgers and peregrine falcons. It is hard to believe that, for 100 years, between the Victorian era and the Second World War, this was the Welsh Klondyke – an unsightly industrial landscape producing over 2 million tons of coal.

things to see and do. It is perfectly possible to spend a whole day there before you even set foot on the Coed Morgannwg Way. The park is open all year, so there are no restrictions on when the walk is done.

From the Visitors' Centre, which is built of local stone and provides information and refreshment, turn right and follow the track as far as the gate, where there is a sign marking the start of the walk. Beyond the gate the way begins a steady, winding ascent through the valley. In fact, quite quickly and surprisingly the path seems to turn its back on the heart of the country park around the Visitors' Centre. This section is clearly for those people keen to explore the wilder stretches of the park on foot. The climb is quite strenuous in places, but as the walk levels out there is a superb vantage point from where much of the country park can be seen, including the upper and lower lakes and, beyond them, the buildings of Cwmdare on the outskirts of Aberdare.

Now you are in wild, uninhabited country, with no signs of civilization whatsoever. From the desolate moorland there are views of distant forests and away to the south, glimpses of the Rhondda valleys. At an old drovers' bridge, the path joins a private road leading up to the Lluest-wen Reservoir. The road follows the edge of the reservoir and then becomes a forest track, cutting between rows of larch trees. The Coed Morgannwg Way keeps to the track until it joins the A4061 road, 4 miles (6 km) to the north of Treherbert. Because of the narrowness of the valley, this little Rhondda town seems to have merged with neighbouring Treorchy, famous for its male-voice choir. This is a common feature of south Wales, where many towns and villages formed an apparently endless chain of mining communities along the valley floors. The valleys were furrows in the bed of a shallow sea that once covered this part of Britain.

The way continues on the other side of the main road, heading in a westerly direction over high ground. At 1,969 feet (598 m) Craig y Llyn is an isolated and windy setting for the start of the next stage of the walk, with magnificent sweeping views over wild moorland and bleak mountains as you look towards the Brecon Beacons National Park.

Craig y Llyn to Afan Argoed Country Park
17 miles (27 km)

After leaving the road, it is worth pausing beside the fence to glance down at the precise, man-made boundaries of Llyn Fawr reservoir among the lines of conifers below. It was built on the site of a prehistoric lake settlement, and an interesting collection of metalwork was discovered from that period. Among the finds was a bronze cauldron, axes and a wrought-iron sickle (which is in the National Museum in Cardiff).

Though the mountains are still clearly visible, the way now heads for the trees that are such a major feature of this walk. After some time there is a sharp change in direction as it begins to head south-west, with woodland scenery on the left of the path and open moorland on the right. Ahead, on the far horizon, there are glimpses of the coastline at Swansea Bay and in the middle distance is a huge rolling carpet of trees. The forests of the Coed Morgannwg Way are a haven for wildlife, with many birds, including ravens and buzzards, to be found in the woods and the wild, upland areas.

This stretch of the way is one of the most delightful, not for its spectacular or extensive views but for the rugged and

Llyn Fawr reservoir is in a spectacular position amid lines of trees below Craig y Llyn, the highest point on the walk.

completely unspoilt landscape through which it runs – a mixture of forest and empty moorland. The path meanders through Forestry Commission land for some distance and here the uniform lines of trees are young sitka spruce – an appropriately tough species of fir for the harsh conditions of this district.

One of the most memorable features of the Coed Morgannwg Way is that it is never far from fast-flowing mountain streams and chattering brooks. Crossing a stream, the way joins a well-defined track through the forest. Soon some quite stunning scenery comes into view away on the right with mountains in the distance. At certain times of the year, particularly in the autumn, the colours of the trees blend superbly to provide a

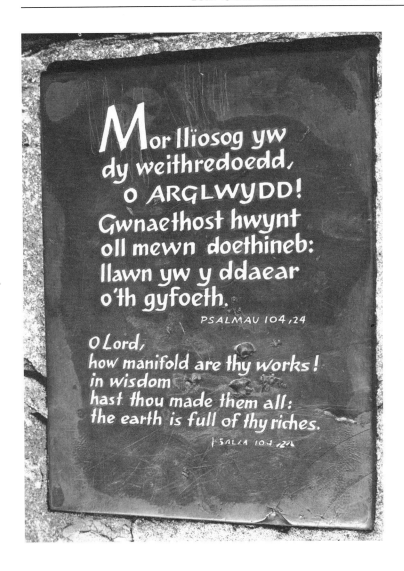

Mor lliosog yw
dy weithredoedd,
o ARGLWYDD!
Gwnaethost hwynt
oll mewn doethineb:
llawn yw y ddaear
o'th gyfoeth.
PSALMAU 104,24

O Lord,
how manifold are thy works!
in wisdom
hast thou made them all:
the earth is full of thy riches.
PSALM 104,24

rich, deep scenic tapestry. With the alpine slopes, the lush green valleys and the streams, this could almost be Austria or Switzerland, such are the vivid beauty and tranquillity of the area.

The way changes direction sharply now and swings into the forest. Very soon it heads south again, but away from the main track, descending steeply through the trees and crossing a gushing stream near the bottom. The path then joins another main forest track at the point where the stream plunges into a waterfall. Gradually the way begins to descend into the Afan valley and then climbs once more at Mynydd Rhiwgregan (*mynydd* is Welsh for mountain), where there are views over three small communities – Abercregan immediately below you,

The dramatic beauty of the surroundings is summed up perfectly by the verse, taken from an evening prayer, on the plaque on the hillside overlooking Llyn Fawr reservoir.

Cymer 1 mile (1.5 km) further along the valley and Duffryn in the other direction to the west, close to the point where the path changes direction again. It is small, remote towns and villages like these which sum up perfectly the flavour and essence of south Wales and its historic mining valleys. The chapels and rows of little houses seem dominated by a spectacular confusion of thickly wooded hills and slopes all around them.

The path continues high above the Afan Valley for some considerable distance. At times the views here are stunning, too, with glimpses of the sea enhancing the picture. Amazingly, the scene before you has been transformed beyond recognition in recent years. Once, much of this valley was the scene of intensive coal mining with working collieries and spoil tips where lines of trees now provide pleasing vistas in all directions.

In a while, the way zigzags down into Afan Argoed Country Park. Beyond the bridge over the River Afan, a large stone by the path commemorates the opening of the Coed Morgannwg Way by the Forestry Commission in 1977 as part of Queen

Opposite The Afan Valley looking towards Abercregan and Cymer. The steep slopes of the valley are now thickly wooded, screening any signs of the coal mining that once dominated this area. Before the Second World War tree planting was carried out by ex-miners, casualties of pit closures.

Shades of Versailles. The splendid orangery at Margam Country Park, little more than a stone's throw from the vast forest of pipes and chimneys at the Port Talbot steelworks, is considered to be the most important eighteenth-century building in South Wales.

Elizabeth II's Silver Jubilee celebrations. As well as providing a picnic and family recreation area with tables and benches arranged around a small playing field, the park offers much more. There are waymarked forest walks and trails, and just off the main A4107 road are the Countryside Centre and Welsh Miners' Museum, which illustrate in a most interesting and entertaining way the history and development of this valley. The park, which has camping facilities, is administered by Glamorgan County Council in association with the Forestry Commission. It is one of a number of amenity areas set up within the 41,000 (101,311 ha) acres of forest to cater for the needs and enjoyment of visitors.

Afan Argoed Country Park to Margam Country Park
13 miles (21 km)

The Coed Morgannwg Way passes beneath the main road and immediately an information board displays a useful map of the overall route of the walk. On the left the maturing oak, cherry, poplar and conifer trees that you see were planted by the children of nearby Cymer Afan School in 1954.

Originally, the site was just an abandoned brickworks but then the Forestry Commission decided to put it to good use by transforming it into their first school forest plot. The project was an outstanding success, giving children an opportunity to learn at first hand about the growth of trees and how they develop in such an environment. This educational facility has since been extended to cover other schools throughout the county.

The way begins a steady climb now, winding through native oak woodland and on towards the summit of Garn Wen. Fortunately, this area of forest managed to escape the massive clearances carried out by local industry during the nineteenth century. At length the path gives way to a superb panoramic view and from Garn Wen, at 1,182 feet (358 m), it is as if the whole of south Wales is spread out beneath you: small towns of chapels and long winding streets, villages, endless mountain scenery and forest – a composite picture of rural and semi-industrial landscapes stretching out into the distance. With good visibility it is possible to see Mumbles Head, Swansea and the Gower from this superb vantage point.

The path soon begins to descend through forested paths and trackways before it emerges into fields. Then it reaches the outskirts of the village of Bryn, which was once a busy coal-mining village with a tramroad. Conveniently there is a pub at this stage of the walk, directly on the route.

The way returns to the quiet of the hills after Bryn and there is quite a steep climb again through the trees. Looking back, though, the views of the valley are splendid. Beside the greens of a golf course on the left, the way changes direction to head south again through forestry land. Keep to the main track and note a stone monument at the verge dedicated to the memory of W. H. (Billy) Vaughan, CBE, of Tailbach near Port Talbot, who was a Forestry Commissioner and, according to the inscription: 'devoted his life and exceptional gifts to the welfare of others. Beloved of all men.'

The way continues to explore the forests and wooded valleys of this area, giving excellent views of Swansea Bay and Margam Country Park below you. The only eyesore is the ugly maze of pipes and chimneys at the Port Talbot Steelworks just beyond Margam. In this area, on the slopes above the country park, are the remains of several Iron Age hillforts.

Port Talbot gets its name from the Talbot family, who lived at Margam Castle. Margam Abbey next door was founded in 1147 by Robert, Earl of Gloucester, and after the Dissolution it was acquired by the Mansel family. The daughter of the first Lord Mansel married John Ivory Talbot of Lacock Abbey and their son subsequently inherited Margam. His heir was Christopher Rice Mansel Talbot and the castle was built for him between 1830 and 1835. Talbot was Liberal MP for Glamorgan from 1830 to 1890, becoming father of the House of Commons during that period, and he was responsible for the early development of Port Talbot.

There are over 800 acres (1.977 ha) of beautiful parkland at Margam, including an immense orangery, built in 1787 which is said to be the largest in the world. With its graceful design and tall, elegant windows, it has often been used as a venue for concerts and other functions over the years. Nearby is the Museum of Early Christian Memorial Stones, containing a number of ancient Celtic crosses which were found close to the route of the walk in the hills above Margam. The park, which is inhabited by deer, sheep and cattle,is an ideal place in which to relax after the rigours of the Coed Morgannwg Way.

BIBLIOGRAPHY
A leaflet describing the route in fairly general terms, with sketches and a map, is available from the Country Parks at either end of the walk:
    Countryside Ranger Office
    Dare Valley Country park
    Aberdare
    Mid Glamorgan CF44 7RG
or
    Margam Country Park
    Margam
    Port Talbot
    West Glamorgan SA13 2TJ

12 The West Mendip Way

Length 30 miles (48 km)
Start Uphill, near Weston-super-Mare
Finish Wells
Going On the whole easy, with several climbs
Ordnance Survey Map 182
Waymarking Oak posts at regular intervals with the use of different coloured arrows: yellow represents a public footpath, blue a bridleway and red is a road

Her Majesty Queen Elizabeth II's Silver Jubilee in 1977 inspired the Rotary Clubs of Weston-super-Mare, Wrington Vale, Mendip and Wells to devise a long-distance footpath linking paths, tracks and bridleways and occasional stretches of road. Two wall plaques at either end of the walk denote that the West Mendip Way was waymarked by the Rotary Clubs and opened on 24 May 1979.

The way will certainly appeal to those who prefer their walking to be leisurely and less challenging than some other paths or to those with not enough time to spare for the longer, more strenuous hikes. It can easily be completed over a weekend or even in a day, and apart from one or two fairly energetic climbs, which give rewarding views over Somerset and the Bristol Channel, it is straightforward and undemanding.

For 30 miles (48 km) it follows the Mendip Hills from the abandoned hill-top church at Uphill on the coast near Weston-super-Mare to the cathedral city of Wells, with Cheddar Gorge and Wookey Hole, the walk's two most famous attractions, in between. Although they merit close inspection for sheer spectacle and natural beauty, the great gorge and the caves are two of the West Country's most commercialized assets and are frequently filled with visitors. Thankfully, there are other less-crowded places to visit – among them the quiet, forgotten village of Priddy, buried high in the hills and home of an annual sheep fair in August, and the splendidly named Crook Peak, one of the landmarks of the Mendips and an outstanding viewpoint.

Wells has much to commend it. Although it is not especially large, it is a dignified city nevertheless, with a winding main street bustling with tourists, most of whom come here to admire the splendours of the cathedral and the fine buildings within its precincts.

Accommodation is generally easy to find at Uphill, Cheddar and Wells and in and around the various villages en route.

There are also good bus and train services at the start of the walk. There is no railway station at Wells, however, but regular bus services depart from here to neighbouring towns and cities.

Uphill to Loxton
7 miles (11 km)

The West Mendip Way begins at Uphill, a residential village a couple of miles or so to the south of Weston-super-Mare (the 'super-Mare' is Latin for 'above the sea', but most people locally just say Weston). With long, sandy beaches, salubrious, invigorating air, numerous stone-built hotels and guesthouses, several piers, fine parks and gardens and a host of other

The ruined roofless church of St Nicholas at Uphill – an appropriate name for such a place. The church, long disused, is still a well-known landmark and the hillock on which it stands signifies the western extremity of the Mendips.

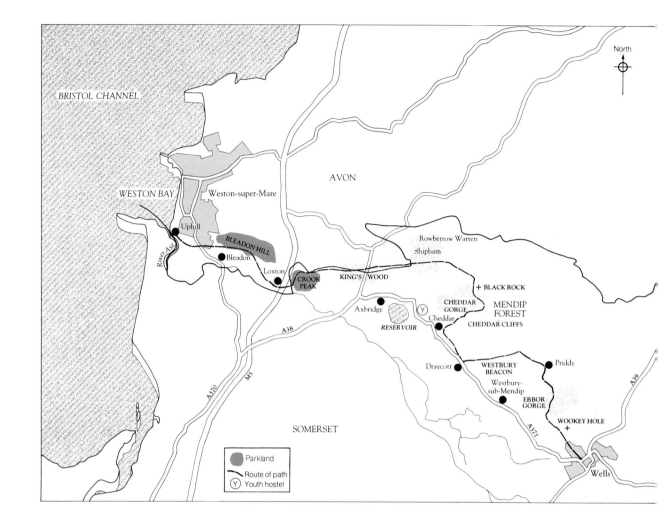

attractions, Weston must qualify as the definitive English holiday resort. Certainly it is the biggest seaside town on the north coast of the West Country.

Uphill lies in the shadow of Weston, but the views from the ancient church of St Nicholas high above the village are magnificent. From the cliff top where the Norman church is situated – though no longer in regular use – you can look across the whole of Uphill, spread out beneath you with Weston and its beaches just beyond.

The hill marks the western end of the Mendip range as it gives way to the mouth of the River Axe, once a Roman port, and then the sea. Immediately below the old church is Uphill Pill – a West Country term for creek or small river – which for a long time was the local harbour. More recently it has become

Standing on the hilltop, it is hard to imagine how some worshippers managed the steep climb to the church, even if the views are so rewarding. A popular local myth suggests that it was when the church was being built at its original site below the cliff, the Devil cunningly removed the stones that were being used and placed them on top of the hill in order to make Christian worship virtually impossible. This explains the village's name – Up-hill. A more likely theory is that the site was chosen because at one time the sea flowed inland here and in all probability the village was also built on this hill top. This version is less interesting, though, and I prefer the legend.

In its time the church has fulfilled other functions as well as being a place of worship. A vigil over the Channel was regularly maintained from the tower and its west wall was once whitewashed as a landmark for shipping. Nowadays a new church serves the village community in a more suitable and accessible location nearby, while St Nicholas remains a sad, conspicuous ruin.

the setting for a boatyard and it is here that the West Mendip Way begins.

Leaving Uphill behind you, the path heads fleetingly for the Axe, frequently filled with stranded boats at low tide, and then changes direction to go away from the coast towards Bleadon. Bypassing the centre of this quiet, hilly village, it climbs on to Bleadon Hill, where the walk then traces the route of an old Roman road, now a quiet country lane crossing the ridge of the hills. The views from here are stunning.

Away to the right can be glimpsed Uphill, the Axe and, on a good day, the Bristol Channel stretching towards Wales. In the foreground the view is predominantly of Somerset's agricultural lowlands, relieved only by Brent Knoll, a rounded hill and local landmark that rises 457 feet (138 m) from the intricate patchwork of fields and was once an island when this entire area was still covered by sea. On top of the hill are the remains of an Iron Age hillfort.

Over on the other side of the narrow road the view is of Weston-super-Mare beyond the fields and trees. Soon the way leaves the road to follow paths and bridleways skirting fields and patches of woodland, the distant hum of traffic across country the only reminder of civilization. Descending gradually into the village of Loxton, there are good views of Crook Peak, with its distinctive cone-shaped summit rising to a height of over 600 feet (182 m) on the near horizon. Loxton lies tucked

Crook Peak. Lofty and distinctive, this landmark is visible for miles around. From the peak the views are tremendous. The Mendips rise from a lowland plain to just over 1,000 (303 m) feet and effectively divide the spirit and character of north-west Somerset.

Opposite The towering splendour of Cheddar Gorge. For almost a mile these limestone cliffs rise vertically above the road, on occasions giving the place a somewhat sinister and oppressive air. Unfortunately, the Gorge is often crammed with visitors who come to admire its unique natural beauty.

away in a gap in the Mendips known as Lox Yeo Valley. The climb to Crook Peak is the start of the next ridge.

Loxton to Cheddar
13 miles (21 km)

The Mendips are 25 miles (40 km) long by about 5 miles (8 km) wide. Chiefly of limestone over old red sandstone, they have a distinctive character and appearance and are not really like any of the other Somerset hills. They are rather severe to look at, wilder and more barren, and in places reminiscent of a primeval landscape.

Crook Peak is one of a chain of medieval beacon sites. Known locally as Crook's Peak, its name is thought to derive from 'cruc', an ancient word which means sharp or pointed hill. Judging from its shape, it is well named. The ground is high and exposed here and even on a summer's day, it can be quite breezy. From the top there are glorious views over large areas of the county. Away to the south and south-west are the Somerset Levels, flat fenland country which is particularly popular with ornithologists and was the setting for the famous Battle of Sedgemoor in 1685. Glastonbury Tor is a distinctive

If a miner wanted to dig for calamine in this area, he would first have to obtain a licence from the Lords Royal. Then, in competition with many others, he would search for a piece of land that had not been worked – judging by the number of mines in existence at Shipham by the end of the eighteenth century, this was not always easy. But mining was a serious business and the men were not easily deterred. Having found some undisturbed ground, the miner would dig a pit about 4 feet (1.2 m) deep before hurling his tools from one side to the other. Where they landed defined the boundaries of his plot, called a 'gruff'. Today, 200 years later, all that remain of this activity are areas of rough, grassy ground.

landmark as you look to the south-east. Rather like Glastonbury, Crook Peak has a curious, almost mystical atmosphere; even when the weather is fine, there is a sinister air about it.

The way continues east from Crook Peak across Wavering Down, with the Avon and Somerset county boundary on your left. It meanders slowly through King's Wood to reach the A38 road, then continues through soft pastoral scenery to the village of Shipham. Beyond it the scenery remains much the same as the way crosses an area of 'gruffy ground' – land which has been worked by miners and dates back mainly to the seventeenth and eighteenth centuries.

Soon you are in Rowberrow Warren, which is Forestry Commission land and was once part of the Royal Forest of Mendip, a favourite hunting ground of kings. Above Rowberrow Warren, to the east, lies Black Down which at 1,068 feet (324 m) is the highest part of the Mendips. Following the signs for Cheddar and Black Down, after Rowberrow the way is mostly over open farmland until you reach Black Rock.

After the gentle rolling country beyond Rowberrow Warren, Black Rock and Cheddar Gorge offer a sharp contrast in scenery, with their dramatic limestone cliffs and splendid caverns. With a little imagination, it is possible to picture how this place must have looked a 100 or more years ago – wild, mysterious and romantic. Today it all seems very different, the result of massive and inevitable commercialization. The Gorge is probably best seen from the top of the cliffs, which rise almost vertically to over 400 feet (121 m) either side of the main road leading to Cheddar village and give frequent and spectacular glimpses of the crags below. If you do not mind crowds, the two main caves, Gough's and Cox's, are worth a visit as they include magnificent illuminated stalactite and stalagmite formations. The village, which is less well known for its strawberries than its cheese, is often crowded with visitors, too, though it is a convenient breaking-off point for refreshment and even an overnight stop.

Cheddar to Wells
10 miles (16 km)

After Cheddar the way goes to Bradley Cross, a small hamlet on the outskirts of the village, and then on to Draycott, a mile or so beyond. The approach to Draycott is over Middle Down Drove, one of the old cattle-drovers' roads, and then across the top of Batcombe Hollow on the south side of Cheddar cliffs. From the village of Draycott on the A371 road it is a steep climb back into the Mendip Hills towards Westbury Beacon, quickly leaving the sights and sounds of traffic and routine village life behind you.

The climb is through spectacular upland country to the highest point of the West Mendip Way, with fields divided by delightful drystone walls and grand views over south Somerset. On a windy day it is one of the most bracing parts of the whole walk.

Beyond the slopes the way reaches the famous Mendip village of Priddy, sheltering in a quiet hollow in the hills. It is a peaceful place, with a collection of houses and cottages and a reputation for clean, purifying air. It was this, together with its remote position high in the Mendips, that led to Priddy becoming the venue for the annual sheep fair in 1348 as the terrible Black Death began to spread rapidly through the

The Victorian paper mill at Wookey Hole.

NICOLA WASTIE

valleys and lowlands of the West Country. Up until then the fair had been held at Wells. Through the centuries the fair has continued to be held here every year on the nearest Wednesday to 21 August, the original date. Symbolic reconstructions of the original sheep hurdles can be seen on the village green.

From Priddy the way is again over farmland until you start to drop down towards Wookey Hole. The descent gives glorious views over the southern slopes of the Mendips as you enter the Ebor Gorge Nature Reserve. This is more wooded than Cheddar Gorge, with a tree-lined path that takes you down into Wookey Hole. The Gorge is by no means as well known as Cheddar and is certainly not as commercialized, being smaller and less accessible. Much of its beauty lies in the fact that it is a peaceful place with no road running through it.

As with Cheddar, Wookey Hole has allowed itself to be exploited by tourism, but it is an interesting place none the less, in a picturesque setting. The Great Cave, with its spectacular stalagmites and stalactites, is worth a visit. The River Axe, curiously blue green colour, flows through it.

The sheep hurdles on the village green at Priddy. Tradition maintains that as long as the symbolic reconstructions remain here, then the annual Priddy fair will continue to take place.

There are other floodlit caverns and tunnels to see. Thousands of years ago they would have been inhabited by wild beasts, such as wolves, giant mammoths and hyenas. There is evidence, too, of Stone Age man living in the caves. Wookey Hole is famous for the legend of the witch. She was supposed to be such an evil character that a monk was sent by the Abbot of Glastonbury to deal with her. He forced her to retreat into the inner caves and there he somehow managed to sprinkle holy water over her, whereupon she immediately turned to stone. The adjoining working Victorian paper mill is also interesting and worth a look.

Out of Wookey Hole you cross through pleasant countryside and up to the summit of a nearby hill known as Arthur's Point (after King Arthur). Another part of the legend of the wicked

The dazzling Bishop's Palace garden offers a glorious vista of Wells Cathedral. The palace is moated and the episcopal swans ring a bell near the drawbridge to demand food.

The west front of Wells Cathedral. Richly decorated with medieval sculptures, the cathedral contains many ancient treasures, including the Lady Chapel and a fourteenth-century clock across the face of which knights joust hourly.

witch of Wookey is that King Arthur plotted her death from here. After Arthur's Point the way passes the open face of Underwood Quarry on the right before reaching the city of Wells. The walk ends on the A39 road, near the buildings of the famous cathedral school.

Wells is one of the smallest – some say the smallest – cities in the country. Certainly it is one of the most elegant, with many

period houses and a fine cathedral that was begun in the latter part of the twelfth century and finished around 200 years later. The cathedral has a most imposing West Front, decorated with medieval sculptures, as its showpiece, but there are many other magnificent features to be admired, the chapter house and the splendid north porch among them.

Vicar's Close, within the cathedral precincts, is a charming street of fourteenth-century houses, and the nearby museum contains some interesting finds from Wookey Hole. A gateway by the cathedral green has the quaint name of Penniless Porch, from the time when beggars used to sit here and collect money from people on their way to the cathedral. Close by is the famous Bishop's Palace, which is thirteenth century in date and moated. The swans here are popular with visitors to the city because they have been trained to ring a roped bell when they are hungry.

BIBLIOGRAPHY
The West Mendip Way, by Andrew Eddy, contains directions, photographs, maps and historical notes, and is available from:
   Woodspring Museum
   Burlington Street
   Weston-super-Mare
   Avon BS23 1PR

Useful Addresses

For general inquiries about Long Distance Paths Advisory
Service (LDPAS) please write to:
 Mr Gerald Cole, Administrator
 Long Distance Paths Advisory Service
 The Barn
 Holme Lyon
 Burneside
 Kendal
 Cumbria LA9 6QX

For specific database inquiries please contact:
 Mr Iain G. Liddell
 Information Officer
 Long Distance Paths Advisory Service
 24 Claremont Court
 Essex Close
 Mount Nod
 Coventry CV4 7HY
 Tel. (day) 0203 523358 (eve.) 0203 466812

★

The Ramblers' Association produces fact sheets listing information about maps, walking equipment and individual paths all
over the country. 'The Ramblers' Yearbook' includes details of
bed and breakfast accommodation and is also published and
updated annually. For general inquiries write to:
 The Ramblers' Association
 1–5 Wandsworth Road
 London SW8 2XX
 Tel. 071–582 6878

★

Countryside Commission
John Dower House
Crescent Place
Cheltenham
Gloucestershire GL50 2RA
Tel. 0242 521381

Countryside Commission
    Office for Wales
Ladywell House
Newtown
Powys SY16 1RD

Countryside Commission for Scotland
Battleby
Redgorton
Perth PH1 3EW
Tel. 0738 27921

★

Camping and Caravanning Club
Greenfields House
Westwood Way
Coventry CV4 8JH
Tel. 0203 694995

The Council for the Protection of Rural England
Warwick House
25 Buckingham Palace Road
London SW1W 0PP
Tel. 071–976 6433

The English Tourist Board
Thames Tower
Blacks Road
Hammersmith
London W6 9EL
Tel. 081–846 9000

The National Trust
36 Queen Anne's Gate
London SW1H 9AS
Tel. 071–222 9251

The National Trust for Scotland
5 Charlotte Square
Edinburgh EH2 4DU
Tel. 031 225 2160

The Scottish Tourist Board
23 Ravelston Terrace
Edinburgh EH4 3EU
Tel. 031 332 2433

The Wales Tourist Board
2 Fitzalan Road
Cardiff CF2 1UY
Tel. 0222 227281

The Youth Hostels Association
(England and Wales)
Trevelyan House
St Stephen's Hill
St Albans
Hertfordshire AL1 2DY
Tel. 0727 55215

The Youth Hostels Association
(Scotland)
7 Glebe Crescent
Stirling FK8 2JA
Tel. 0786 51181

Illustration Credits

The publisher and author would like to thank the following:

Chapter One – The Two Moors Way. All photographs by Forbes Stephenson.

Chapter Two – The Isle of Wight Coastal Path. All photographs by Eric A. Cross.

Chapter Three – The Vanguard Way. Pages 61, 64: R.S. Frankham; page 65: M. Godber; pages 67, 68, 69, 73, 76: Joyce and Maurice Flower.

Chapter Four – The Suffolk Coast Path. Pages 81, 84, 85: G.D. Oliver; page 87: John D. Mummery; page 88: D.R. Leak; pages 90, 91, 92: John D. Mummery; page 93: D.R. Leak.

Chapter Five – The Yoredale Way. All photographs by Digby J. Angus.

Chapter Six – The Wear Valley Way. All photographs by C.G. Banks.

Chapter Seven – The Speyside Way. Pages 132, 133, 136: Jim Strachan; page 139: the author; pages 140, 141: Jim Strachan; page 142: the author.

Chapter Eight – The Calderdale Way. Pages 145, 147, 149, 151: J. Sutcliffe; page 153: R.S. Cunliffe; pages 155, 156: J. Sutcliffe.

Chapter Nine – Glyndwr's Way. Page 160: John Evans; page 161, 163: Pauline Horton; page 167: Steven Williams; page 168: John Evans; page 171: Brian Pollard; page 173: Brian Pollard (black and white), Chris Townsend (colour).

Chapter 10 – The Heart of England Way. All photographs by John Cartlidge, A.R.P.S.

Chapter 11 – The Coed Morgannwg Way. All photographs by W.A. Stuart-Jones.

Chapter 12 – The West Mendip Way. Page 205: B.L.J. Young; page 208; D.L. Overton; page 209: D.L.J. Young; pages 212, 213, 214: D.L. Overton.

Index

Page numbers in *italic* refer to illustrations.